THE PARADOX OF PERFECTION

THE PARADOX OF PERFECTION

HOW EMBRACING OUR
IMPERFECTION PERFECTS US

Jeffrey S. Reber, PhD, LPC
Steven P. Moody, LCSW

CrossLink Publishing

CrossLink Publishing
1601 Mt. Rushmore Rd., Ste 3288
Rapid City, SD 57701
www.crosslinkpublishing.com

Ordering Information:
Quantity sales. Special discounts are available on quantity purchases by corporations, associations, and others. For details, contact the "Special Sales Department" at the address above.

The Paradox of Perfection/Reber & Moody —1st ed.

ISBN 978-1-63357-152-5

Library of Congress Control Number: 2018948431

First edition: 10 9 8 7 6 5 4 3 2 1

All scripture quotations are taken from the Holy Bible, King James Version (Public Domain).

<u>About the Cover</u>
Kintsugi (or "golden seams") is a centuries old art form that embraces the Japanese aesthetic philosophy of *Wabi Sabi*, which emphasizes the beauty of imperfection. Lacquer masters fill the cracks in broken ceramics with a golden lacquer that is sanded and polished until the joint is even and seamless, making the object whole and enhancing its beauty, strength, and value.

To our wives and our children, with whom we have been blessed to share precious moments of God's perfect love.

Contents

Introduction

We begin with a confession: We are perfectionists. It is not easy to admit this publicly. Indeed, it is even harder to own up to the fact that we have often been perfectionistic as we have written this very book, which is designed to counteract perfectionism. These admissions are difficult for us, in part because perfectionism is itself an imperfection. It exposes a flaw in our character, and like all perfectionists, we do not want to have weaknesses and flaws—and we certainly do not want other people to know about them!

On the contrary, even though we know better, even though we know flawlessness is a fantasy, we still want you to think we are perfect. In fact, we would like you to think that we just sat down in front of a computer, that a conduit of insight opened in our minds, and that we wrote this book in a few days as a single draft with no mistakes and no revisions in the process. Like so many of you, we want to appear as if everything comes naturally and easily to us, as if we are the Mozarts of book writing. Then we get to look like geniuses and you get to read a book that is flawless in its treatment of this critical issue. Could anything feel better than that?

The fact of the matter is that it has taken us years to create this book. We have written, revised, and rewritten the manuscript many times over. We have thrown out entire chapters, and we have labored over every single word. We have not seen eye to eye on every topic and theme, and we have run drafts by trusted colleagues and friends who have pointed out minor flaws that have led us—true to our perfectionistic tendency to catastrophize—to question whether we were even capable of writing a book at all. We have felt incompetent, and we have considered giving up on this project many times.

In short, our perfectionism nearly sabotaged the publication of this book on perfectionism on several occasions! This is not an indictment of the book. On the contrary, we think this book contains several valuable insights and will be of use to many people. But it is not perfect. Like us, this book is flawed.

We have chosen to acknowledge these flaws in ourselves and our book, despite the hit our egos will take for it, to counter a cultural tendency toward the pretense of perfection. Perfectionism has perpetuated itself for so long and so successfully in our culture precisely because it leads so many people to prop up a facade of perfection (just look at any social media outlet, if you doubt this), and it forces into hiding the real feelings and thoughts we experience and from which so many of us suffer. It keeps us from talking honestly with each other about our flaws and our faults, and it engenders a false belief that others do not have imperfections or somehow do not struggle with their own imperfections the same way we do.

We cannot tell you how many times we have sat with clients in therapy who lament, "Why can't I be like so-and-so? They don't have all these problems. They always have their act together. They are practically perfect." Little do they know that the very person they think is almost perfect was just in our office the day before, lamenting all their inadequacies, feeling like a failure, and comparing themselves to other people who appear perfect to *them*.

Despite the pressure to keep our weaknesses private, we hope you will participate with us in honestly and frankly reflecting upon our shared weakness of perfectionism, as well as the individual forms it takes in each of our lives. Such a genuine reflection will only succeed if we are communicating with the real you, the whole you,—not only the you that you present to the world or the you that you would like to present to yourself, but also the you that tries to be completely honest with yourself and does not try to hide from aspects of yourself that are uncomfortable or embarrassing.

This honesty will take some effort because, as you will see in chapters 1 and 2, it is easy to deny perfectionism at a conscious level, while still clinging to it in the deepest recesses of our minds, hearts, and culture. Indeed, we know from our own experience how often we say the words to ourselves and others, "Well, nobody's perfect!" and we know how hard people work to convince themselves and others that they really believe what they are saying: that imperfection is okay; that it is normal to be an imperfect person, to have an imperfect marriage, to parent imperfectly, and to be a member of an imperfect community.

But if you are like us, that is not the whole story. It is not quite the true story. If you are like us, the real you thinks, "Yes, nobody's perfect, but it would sure be a better world if everyone was perfect, or at least if I was perfect. In fact, I ought to be the exception to the rule. My marriage and my family ought to be the exception to the rule, as well. At the very least, my church should be perfect. Perfection should be possible. If I just work harder at it, I should be able to get there. If perfection is not truly possible, though, I should at least make it appear as if it is, as if I have somehow achieved it, in order to save face among my peers."

We warn you against these often subconscious forms of resistance to honest self-reflection, for they are at the heart of what we describe here as the "double bind of perfectionism": First, as we will discuss in chapter 2, our perfectionism binds us to an ever-present painful awareness of the considerable distance between the ideal and ourselves. And second, we are bound by our perfectionism to maintain the appearance of perfection in order to save face in a culture in which perfection is so highly valued, knowing all the while that it is a mere facade. This contradiction between awareness and appearance leads us to feel like we are always imposters who could be exposed as frauds at any moment.

Walking into church on Sunday morning, then, requires a considerable "gearing up" for the event. Our dress and grooming must be just so. Our children must be reminded not to embarrass us with any unruly behavior. We must put on our best smiles even if the world feels like it is crashing down around us. And into the church we go, fearing more than anything that someone will see us as we really are and judge us, criticize us, or otherwise expose our weakness to the world.

Constantly trying to hide imperfections from others is exhausting and painful. The idea of voluntarily sharing faults and failings with others quite frankly scares perfectionists to death. This deathly fear is understandable. Sharing our frailty openly with others is taking a step into uncharted territory, for few of us do so regularly and we do not know how others will respond. However, as disciples of Christ, we do not have much of a choice. As we will discuss in greater detail in chapter 3, the path of discipleship, the walk of Christ, is one in which weaknesses are not only identified, but also shared and ultimately embraced.

Consider many of the stories described in the Bible in which, the weaknesses of prophets and kings, of fathers and mothers, of sons and daughters are all laid bare before the entire world. When Moses was denied entry into the promised land because of his disobedience, not only did the children of Israel learn of it, but so, too, do each of us when we read about it in the Scriptures. When Jonah tried to run from God's command to call the people of Ninevah to repentance, we are all there as readers to witness his decision to flee. When Job cried out that God "uproots my hope like a tree" (Job 19:10 niv), his despair and frustration over his suffering is not kept private. All of it is shared in all its nitty-gritty detail over the course of forty-two chapters. When Samson succumbed to Delilah's temptation and lost his hair, his strength, and his vision, his slipup is not hidden from our sight.

Similarly, David's sins of adultery and conspiracy to murder are exposed, as is Solomon's pride and Saul's fall from grace. Isaiah confesses his lack of eloquence, Paul admits to a "thorn in my flesh" (2 Corinthians 12:7 niv), and Peter loses his faith as he tries to walk on water and eventually denies knowing Christ three times. Thomas doubts the witness of the resurrected Christ given by the other apostles. Martha fails to choose "what is better" (Luke 10:40–42 niv). Fearing what is to come, Christ Himself asks God to let the cup of the sins of all humanity pass from Him just before He submits to His Father's will.

The Bible certainly is not an account of flawlessness. It does not even remotely uphold the pretense of perfection. On the contrary, it openly violates the social norm prohibiting the public sharing of our weaknesses on nearly every page. In it we read story after story of sins committed, disobedience and rebellion manifested, repentance undertaken, forgiveness extended, weakness demonstrated yet again and again, and failure repeated, etc. If God's holy writ does not allow His own beloved prophets to save face, but instead reveals their weaknesses and faults to all generations of people who have read or will read the Bible, then why should we expect anything different for ourselves in our much-less-broadly-publicized lives?

We make the case in chapters 4, 5, and 6 that we should not try to hide our failings and flaws from our partners, our families, or our congregations, for they are the means by which a truly communal perfection in Christ can be achieved. We even go so far as to suggest in chapter 7 the broader societal and perhaps even global impact that might result if weaknesses were shared and embraced rather than despised and hidden. Ultimately, we conclude this book with the assertion that it is not flawlessness or the pretense of perfection that perfects us. It is our weakness, frailty, flaws, and even sinfulness that give Christ's perfecting love and redemption access to us and in turn provide us access to His divine mercy and grace.

But none of this can ever get off the ground if we, the authors, do not admit to our perfectionism right off the bat, and if we do not publicly acknowledge and even "glory in" (2 Corinthians 12:9 kjv) our weakness and infirmities with you and with our God. This book also will not succeed if you, the reader, will not openly and honestly admit to your perfectionism, first to yourself as you privately read along with us, but most importantly to your God and then also to your partner, your family, and to your "fellowcitizens" (Ephesians 2:19 kjv) of the faith. It will be hard for us and it will be hard for you, but in the end our admission and acceptance of weaknesses and faults, including the weakness of perfectionism, will bring us closer to our Savior and allow us to receive His loving embrace. Indeed, through our weaknesses, we will become yoked to Christ in a relational perfection that makes flawed beings "perfect, even as your Father which is in heaven is perfect" (Matthew 5:48 kjv), and not just in the next life, but here and now in this mortal sphere.

CHAPTER 1

Perfect and Christian?

Christian perfection is not, and never can be, human perfection.

—Oswald Chambers

Please read through the following features of perfectionism and put a checkmark next to any item that applies to you most of the time:

_____ I often feel guilty when I make a mistake.

_____ Failure is not an option.

_____ Nothing feels worse than knowing that something I did wrong caused another person to suffer.

_____ The world would be a better place if everyone did everything right.

_____ God is happier with me when I commit fewer sins.

_____ I rarely feel truly good about myself.

_____ I tend to focus on the flaws that I can see in myself and/or others.

_____ I believe society is better off when people pursue perfection.

_____ I have used the words "nobody's perfect" to console myself or someone else.

_____ If it was possible, living a life without sin would be the best kind of life to live.

_____ I would like to be free of my weaknesses.

_____ I know I am making progress in life if I am reducing the number of errors and failures I commit.

So, how did you do? Did you get a perfect score of 100 percent? If so, do you really think it is a good thing to get a perfect score on a perfectionism quiz? We will give you a moment to ponder that conundrum. Seriously, though, if you placed a checkmark next to all or most of these statements, what does that mean? It does not necessarily mean that you are a perfectionist (though you may be). It does mean, however, that, like most people in our Western culture, you speak what we refer to in this book as the "language of perfectionism." And like most people, it is likely the primary, if not the only language you know. We will have more to say about the dominance of the language of perfectionism a little later. For now, we want to be sure that you understand the major theme of this language, which we label here the "fantasy of flawlessness."

The Fantasy of Flawlessness

The fantasy of flawlessness consists of four parts: 1) the concept of perfection that is commonly used in American culture, which is defined as being free of faults or as having the characteristic of flawlessness (Schwartz, 2008); 2) the relentless pursuit of flawlessness coupled with an intolerance for error in oneself and/or others (Howard, 2011); 3) the measuring of self-worth and well-being according to the success of one's pursuit of flawlessness (Sturman, Flett, Hewitt, Rudolph, 2009); and 4) never feeling truly good about oneself because flawlessness is an ideal that inevitably eludes us all. For so-called adaptive perfectionists—a term we find very problematic for reasons that will become more clear as we go—falling short of the ideal motivates a greater striving for goals, higher standards, and a redoubling of one's efforts. "Maladaptive" perfectionists, on the other hand, despair over the distance between themselves and their perceived ideal, experience hopelessness, and manifest a number of neuroses.

There can be little doubt that at a societal level, the pursuit of the fantasy of flawlessness has yielded impressive results. IQ scores increase every year (Flynn, 2007). Technology has advanced at breakneck speed (Barton, 2013). We are wealthier than ever before, and we have extended our life expectancies and increased the quality of our lives many-fold. However, despite being smarter, being healthier, being more beautiful, and having greater material wealth and more technological conveniences than ever before, we are no happier, no more satisfied with our marriages and our families, and no less worried than the generations that lived more flawed lives before us.

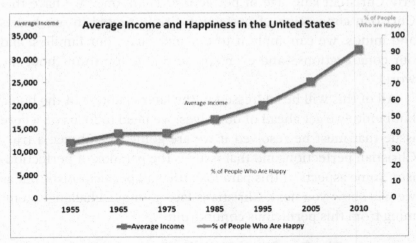

Data Source: *Historical Statistics of the United States and Economic Indicators*

On the contrary, anxiety and depression are at an all-time high, as is obesity, divorce, the abuse and neglect of children, and suicide. Stress has become chronic for most people, and it arises at earlier ages of life than ever before, contributing to increases in heart disease, high blood pressure, and stroke.

We could go on and on here, but our purpose is not to bring you down. Quite the opposite. The goal of this book is to replace despair with hope, by showing you that a genuine perfection is achievable right here and right now, in this life, even for flawed and fallen beings. But in order for us to be able to embrace this achievable perfection and apply it to our lives, we have to clear a space in our hearts and minds for it.

We must recognize that the conception of perfection as flawlessness that dominates our current ways of thinking is not the only kind of perfection. Most importantly for Christians, it is not the perfection that Christ intended when He commanded us to "be ye therefore perfect, even as your father which is in heaven is perfect" (Matthew 5:48 kjv). To achieve the form of perfection that Christ commands of us, we must learn a new, properly Christian language of perfection. Then, once we have that Christian conception of perfection firmly rooted in our hearts and minds, we can apply it to our marriages, our families, and our congregations—and even spread perfection throughout the world.

All of this will be addressed in the later chapters of the book, but before we get ahead of ourselves, we need to focus on a core issue that must be resolved if we are going to embrace a truly Christian perfection, and that issue is the paradox of perfectionism. Some aspects of this paradox afflict all perfectionists, but as we will show you next, Christians face a unique challenge stemming from this pernicious conundrum.

The Paradox of Christian Perfectionism

To understand this core issue, we need to frame the fantasy of flawlessness that drives perfectionism in Christian terms. For the Christian, perfection is embodied in Jesus Christ. Christ was the only being to ever walk the earth who lived a blameless life in which every action, every word, every thought, and every feeling was entirely without fault. With Christ there was no second-guessing, no regrets, and no guilt or shame. When Christ threw over the tables of the moneychangers on the temple grounds, there was no loss of control or error of temperament. It was the perfect thing to do because God did it, and as God, Christ stands blameless before any accusations of a lost temper and wrongdoing. There is no fault in Him, so nothing can be wrong with what He did. It was exactly as it should be—no more, no less.

Whether we are conscious of it or not, perfectionists desire that same certainty. We want to know that our actions are perfectly suited to the context and are without flaw. We want there to be no fault in us—ever. Only then, when we are perfect, just as Christ is perfect, will we be satisfied. The problem is that if this fantasy of flawlessness were to somehow come true, we would not need Christ, not only because we would commit no sins nor make any mistakes for which His grace and mercy are required, but also because we would have become Christs unto ourselves, that is, beings who live a perfect life and are basically gods themselves.

If the fantasy of flawlessness were to come true, then Christ could not forgive our failures, because we would have no shortfalls. He could not strengthen us, because we would have no weaknesses. He could not redeem us because we would have no sins. We would be self-sufficient. We would essentially be gods unto ourselves.

Because flawlessness negates our dependency upon Christ, Christians are faced with a tough question: What do we really want? Do we ultimately want blamelessness? Do we want the certainty of faultless actions? Do we want complete freedom from blemish, weakness, and wrongdoing? Do we want to be gods ourselves? Or do we ultimately want God? Do we want to depend on Him who is without blemish, to rely wholly upon His mercy and grace, His love and compassion? Do we want to be in relationship with the Being who lived a perfect life, who is without blame or fault, who extends His hands to us, who seeks to yoke Himself to us so that He can raise us up, hold us close, and make us one with Him?

In your heart of hearts, at the end of the day, you must decide what you want most: Christ or flawlessness. You cannot ultimately have both. If you are flawless, then you have no need of Christ. If you have Christ, then it is because you are flawed and you depend upon Him. You must choose one or the other, perfectionism or Christianity. You cannot ultimately be both a Christian and a perfectionist for "No man can serve [those] two masters" (Matthew 6:24 kjv). So, which is it: Christ or flawlessness?

Before you answer this most important of questions, consider this critical complication: Recall that Christ, our Master, whom we love dearly and want to follow in every way, commanded His disciples to "be ye therefore perfect, even as your father which is in heaven is perfect" (Matthew 5:48 kjv). Christian perfectionists (an oxymoron that we will tolerate for now), then, are not pursuing flawlessness because it is something they decided would be a good goal for their lives or a better master than Christ. They pursue it precisely because they believe the God whom they worship has commanded them to do so. They feel compelled to pursue a flawless life as a matter of discipleship.

This, then, is the paradox of Christian perfectionism: The Being whom we pursue as our Lord and Master appears to have commanded us to pursue flawlessness, but if we pursue flawlessness, it inevitably leads us away from our Lord and Master. We have already mentioned one way in which this paradox plays out, which is that if we were somehow able to keep Christ's commandment to be flawless, we would have no need of Christ, because we would be sinless, just as He is sinless, all on our own. *Our flawlessness, in this case, would perfect us right out of our relationship with Christ.*

A second possibility, one that is more likely, is that our efforts to keep Christ's commandment to be perfect by living flawlessly will always fall short, because we are not Christ and we do not have His divine capacity to live without fault. Because of this, we remain perpetual violators of one of God's commandments, and as a result we cannot help but remain sinful. And as unrepented sinners, we are then not worthy of Christ's redemption. *Our sinfulness, in this case, would imperfect us right out of our relationship with Christ.*

So, either our perfection separates us from our Lord, or our imperfection separates us from our Lord. This is a genuine paradox, and it raises a most troubling question: Why would Christ, who has commanded us to come unto Him, also command us to pursue something that would ultimately lead us away from Him?

Consequences of Christian Perfectionism

Confusion and Frustration

As you can imagine, and as you may have experienced in your own life, this paradox of perfectionism creates a great deal of confusion and frustration for people who earnestly seek to follow Christ and obey His commandments. The experience of a woman named Katie demonstrates a prototypical case of this confusion:

> I was feeling the need to be perfect. Since I could never attain what I thought "perfection" looked like, I would get discouraged and think, why even try? Because of my imperfections, I was certain God would never bless me, or never answer any of my prayers, because those are only things He does for righteous people. And since I was so imperfect, there was no way that could happen for me.
>
> On top of that, I would constantly feel guilty, and my guilt had turned into one where my actions were based on a foundation of guilt and the idea that God was

> disappointed in me because I was never doing enough,
> but at the same time, I was too exhausted to do more
> than I already was (Younger, 2016).

Katie was clearly caught in the paradox of perfectionism. Her "need to be perfect" led her away from God, not toward Him, because she believed flawlessness was a prerequisite for God's love and blessings, and she could never satisfy that prerequisite. And why wouldn't she believe that? Perfection is a commandment from God, and a good Christian is to keep God's commandments (John 14:15). If we do not keep God's commandments, then we are committing sin (1 John 3:4). If we commit sin, we must repent and forsake, or "lay aside," the sin (Proverbs 28:13; Hebrews 12:1). If we do not forsake the sin, we will continue to violate God's commandment and live in sin, even unto spiritual death (Romans 6). But we cannot lay aside the sin of our imperfection when none of us can live a flawless life. Consequently, no matter how hard we try to repent and forsake the sin of our imperfection, it will always be there in us and we will never be "born of God" (1 John 3:9) or able to "walk in newness of life" (Romans 6:4). This is why Katie felt so unworthy of God's love, answers to prayers, and blessings. She fully believed she was separated from God by the sin of imperfection, which she could not lay aside because she could not achieve a flawless life.

Contradictory Counsel

Do Katie's concerns sound familiar? Perhaps you have personally experienced thoughts and feelings just like Katie's. Or maybe a member of your family or a good friend has expressed these kinds of worries to you. If so, can you recall what you said, either to yourself or to them, to aid in coping with the burden of perfectionism? Was the advice helpful? Did it console you or the other person, and were you or they able to find relief and hope? Most importantly, did your counsel result in a stronger relationship with Jesus Christ and embolden faith in Him unto salvation?

We are sure that you, like us, would like to be able to answer those last three questions with a resounding "yes!" At the very least, we would like to be able to say that our counsel did not make the problem worse. Surely none of us would knowingly do anything to weaken a person's relationship with the Savior. We all only want to help. But perfectionism, as we have shown already, is a pernicious concept, and the confusion it creates can find its way into even the most compassionate counsel and altruistic advice. Our efforts to console others can even unintentionally reinforce the paradox of perfectionism in ourselves and others as we attempt to resolve it.

To assess the extent of this potential problem, we have examined hundreds of Internet postings consisting of counsel to perfectionists and we have asked dozens of people, including several pastors and other Church leaders, to share the advice they would give to someone like Katie who struggles with perfectionism as a Christian. Our investigation yielded two major conclusions. First, most Christians (and many people of other faiths and backgrounds) have very similar feelings and advice about how to cope with perfectionism. Second, most of the feelings and advice on which people rely to cope with perfectionism inevitably and unknowingly reinforces the very perfectionism the advice-givers seek to resolve. In what follows, we will briefly review six common themes that pervade the advice people offer to perfectionists, and we will demonstrate how the advice unintentionally supports one or more features of the paradox of perfectionism.

Theme #1: "Nobody's perfect!"

Almost without fail, every person who wrote a comment on the Internet or who responded to our direct question concerning the advice they would offer to perfectionists initiated their advice by telling the perfectionist in more or less the same words that "nobody's perfect." Surely, these words are designed to console perfectionists by letting them know that we are all in the same boat together. However, this attempt at consolation will provide little comfort to the perfectionist, if the boat we are all in together is sinking! Saying that none of us can keep Christ's commandment to be perfect means that all of us are disobedient and living in sin. If misery truly does love company, perhaps there is some solace to be found in our shared awful fate, but this will hardly help someone like Katie to feel better. Instead, she will now feel just as badly for all of us as she does for herself. She will also likely wonder what kind of a God would issue a commandment that no one can obey. That does not feel like something a loving, merciful God would do. It certainly does not seem very Christian!

Theme #2: Perfection is a goal, not an expectation.

A second theme that figured prominently in the advice we found on the Internet and in our direct questioning was the assertion that God does not actually expect us to keep His commandment to be perfect as our Father in heaven is perfect. As one Church leader put it, "Perfection is something we are asked to strive for but are not expected to obtain in mortality." This counsel is surely intended to ease the mind of the perfectionist (or at least the mind of the person giving the advice!). However, the perfectionist will easily see right through it, as one self-proclaimed perfectionist did in an online comment: "Jesus said 'be perfect,' not 'become perfect' like the heavenly Father. He commanded mortal man to be exalted Gods" (Rich, 2013). The comment may strike you as a bit extreme, but that does not make its basic premise wrong. Christ did command us to *be* perfect, not to *become* perfect or to *strive for* perfection—and wouldn't "being perfect" mean being flawless, just like an exalted god? How, then, does this counsel not lead someone like Katie to see it as a reinterpretation or even a distortion of God's words, designed to make people feel better about consistently coming up short?

There is another considerable problem with this second theme: Think what it would mean if we treated all of God's commandments as goals to strive for rather than expectations. What would "Thou shalt not kill" mean if it was understood in this way? "Please, strive not to kill others? Try to become non-homicidal? You are not really expected to pull it off but do your best." Or what about "Thou shalt not commit adultery"? Can a husband who just cheated on his wife come home and say he tried his hardest not to cheat, so it is okay? Should he and his wife acknowledge that he may never be able to be loyal in this lifetime, but in the next life he will finally be able to honor his marriage vows? And does the wife (or God, for that matter) have to accept that his striving for the goal of fidelity will be realized in eternity rather than expect fidelity in their marriage right here and now in mortality?

Obviously, if this counsel—that we are not actually command-ed to be perfect, but need only to strive for it—was applied to all of God's commandments, then we would find ourselves on a very slippery slope. If, on the other hand, this counsel is supposed to be applied only to the commandment to be perfect, then on what grounds is that exclusion justified? Why is the commandment to be perfect the exception to the rule? Aren't we supposed to obey *all* of God's commandments here and now in this life, and aren't we going to be judged according to our obedience to the com-mandments in mortality?

Theme #3: Come unto Christ and He will perfect you.

A third theme that emerged regularly in the advice we re-viewed was the idea that we can become perfect through Christ. This rings true to many Christians. If Christ commanded us to be perfect and we can't be perfect on our own, then He must be the One who makes us perfect. The problem with this is that many perfectionists have tried to implement Christ's perfection in their lives, but it always seems to fail. They have accepted

Christ and acknowledged their dependence upon Him, repented of their sins, and given their will over to Him, but after doing all that, they still make mistakes, they still commit sins, and they are still flawed. Their weaknesses still feel like weaknesses, just as they did before, and they are still racked with guilt and feelings of inadequacy. Where is the perfection? Where is the flawlessness? How can we keep the commandment to be perfect, even through Christ, if we remain imperfect, just as we always have been? If, in response to this dilemma, we tell ourselves and others, like Katie, that our perfection through Christ will come in the next life, then we fall right back into the quagmire we just discussed in theme #2.

Furthermore, even if we could achieve flawlessness through Christ, a second issue is still at play: This appears to place Christ in the position of being the means to our end. Flawlessness is the ultimate goal, and Christ's job is to help us achieve it. As one advice-giver put it in her attempt to console other perfectionists: "We have to rely on Christ to make us perfect for now, until we can be perfect by ourselves in the next life" (personal communication, May 22, 2016). Our dependency on Christ, then, is temporary, merely a mortal placeholder until our individual perfection can be achieved in the next life on our own. Then, once we have attained that state of perfection independently, we won't need Christ anymore. How can someone like Katie, or any of us for that matter, understand that the Lord is the "alpha and the omega, the beginning and the end" (Revelation 1:8; 22:13) when advice like this suggests that flawlessness is the true end and Christ is only a temporary means to that end?

Theme #4: All we can do is our best, and Christ will take care of the rest.

This commonly expressed theme is related to theme #3, but it has its own unique challenge for the perfectionist (and if you are one, you surely already know what it is). The challenge is that the perfectionist reads, "Do your best," and interprets those words as "Do everything and do it right." For the perfectionist, doing your best and being perfect are synonyms, so when you try to console perfectionists by telling them to do all they can, you are essentially telling them to be flawless, and only reinforcing their frustration over falling short of that ideal.

This advice also suggests to perfectionists that our part in perfection is separate from Christ's part. We must take care of our side of things, "doing our best", and then Christ will take care of His side, "making up the rest." And what is our side of things? Keeping the commandments, which includes the commandment to be perfect as our Father in heaven is perfect. So, we come full circle to a commandment we cannot keep, and in the process of giving this advice we have only reinforced the perfectionists' feeling that they must somehow do it all and they must do it all by themselves.

Theme #5: The devil is the source of discouragement and guilt about being imperfect.

People who give advice to perfectionists commonly try to reassure them by asserting that the negative feelings they experience about falling short of perfection do not come from God and are not His will. As one well-intended advice-giver put it:

> Satan . . . makes us feel guilty that we're not doing enough. As a result, he makes us feel unworthy of God's help and blessings. And sometimes he's successful in making us feel so guilty that he can discourage us from even feeling worthy to communicate with God.

But this attempt at reassurance is confusing for perfectionists like Katie, because the perfectionist is struggling with things that *God* has said about perfection and commanded of us, not what the devil has said. In Matthew 5:48, it was Christ who issued the commandment for us to be perfect like our Father in heaven, not

Satan, so why is the devil to blame when we feel badly for breaking this commandment? Isn't guilt the proper feeling we should have when we sin? Doesn't that guilt motivate us to repent, forsake the sin, and begin to do better? The guilt seems more likely to come from God as a signal to us of our sin and need for repentance than as a lie whispered into our ears by the devil. In fact, if the devil is consistent, it would be more likely that he would try to deceive us into thinking that we don't have to keep God's commandments at all (recall how he tempted Eve to take the fruit), including the commandment to be perfect.

Theme #6: Perfection actually means being whole, complete, and finished.

A final common theme in the advice given to perfectionists focuses on the translation of the word perfect in Matthew 5:48. A number of advice-givers note that the word used in the original Greek does not connote "flawlessness," but rather completion and wholeness. As one respondent to our direct question put it:

> Perfect means "complete, finished, fully developed." When I think of perfection in these terms, then it's easier for me to understand I don't have to (and won't!) be perfect right now. That as a child of God, I am still learning, and growing, and developing. And that is as it should be! If we came to Earth perfect, there would be no need for a Savior or the Atonement.

This advice-giver correctly notes that if we were perfect we would not need Christ, but she mistakenly falls prey to the issue we discussed in theme #2. Whether perfection is defined as completion and wholeness or flawlessness and freedom from faults, we are commanded to be perfect here and now in this life. Making oneself complete and fully finished or becoming whole and fully developed through Christ in mortality is just as insurmountable a task as making oneself flawless or free of faults through Christ.

It doesn't matter which of these two definitions is used. Trading one impossible ideal for another is cold comfort to perfectionists and leaves the questions at the heart of the paradox of perfectionism firmly in place: Why would Christ command us to do something we cannot do, and why would He command us to do something that inevitably leads us away from Him?

Is There No Other Way?

After reading through these common themes, you may wonder why so much of the advice people offer to perfectionists falls short and even reinforces the paradox of perfectionism, when their desire is surely to help perfectionists feel better, have greater hope, and grow closer to Christ. How is it that both perfectionists and the people who seek to console them seem to fall prey so often to the fundamental paradox that perfectionism creates? Perhaps it is because at some level we know there is no way out of the paradox of perfectionism and we are just trying to sugarcoat a bitter pill that we all inescapably must swallow. One frustrated respondent to an online discussion in which people tried to console perfectionists by using several of the themes we have reviewed here, seems to think this is so:

> Let's just call a spade a spade here. When perfection is the goal, the end result is and always will be failure. Holding the myth of perfection up as the standard of thought and action means that one can NEVER measure up, EVER! Nothing one does will ever be good enough, no matter what it is. Every little mistake, every minute oversight, every perceived misstep weighs heavily on the mind of a person who demands perfection of themselves and who feels that others expect it of him/her. The guilt of being consistently imperfect leads to an incessant cycle of confession, repentance, and misery. While the intent of this belief may be to

motivate people to reach higher and achieve more, it also creates feelings of bitter disappointment and self-recrimination. Over time, as the expectation of perfection is repeatedly reinforced, these feelings of inadequacy become deeply entrenched and a pattern of self-loathing emerges. Striving for perfection is a form of poison. It is strychnine for self-esteem (Lucyfer, 2007).

Is this comment true? Is there really no way out of this paradox? Do we either have to be honest with ourselves and others about the commandment to be perfect and become completely depressed and alienated from God as a result of our inevitable failure to keep it, like Katie was? Or do we have to deceive ourselves by pretending that God didn't really command us to be perfect, even though He clearly did? Is there no other way? We believe there is, but before we can discuss this other way, we ask you to join us in taking a few minutes to consider how we have come to find ourselves in the troubling position we are in, a paradoxical position in which it seems as if there is no other way to live and/or speak as a Christian, but perfectionistically. As you will see in the next chapter, there are intellectual and emotional forces that drive the paradox of perfectionism and have led so many people to speak the language of perfectionism and that language alone.

CHAPTER 2

The Language of Perfectionism

*I think it's unfortunate that we have evolved into a language
in which we talk about perfectionism as "adaptive."*

—Randy Frost

In a very real sense, our minds are not our own, at least
not completely. Much of your individual mind comes to
you from outside yourself. For example, the language you
are using to think as you read these words and interpret their
meaning was not created by you in your head. You were not
born with the language you speak. It was taught to you by parents, siblings, teachers, and books, and it became internalized
to such a deep level that now your thoughts simply show up in
terms of the language. Your language and your thoughts have
become one and the same.

Language is one key component of the sociocultural context
that helps form your mind, a very obvious component, but there
are many other aspects of your culture that have also become
part of your mind and are now seemingly indistinguishable from
your own thoughts and ideas. Given the long history of perfectionism in our culture and the many ways in which it is taught
to us and reinforced by parents, teachers, churches, and the media, we would suggest that perfectionism, like the languages we

speak, has become a deeply ingrained component of the minds of many people.

This means that perfectionistically minded people do not have experiences and then translate those experiences into the terms and meanings of perfectionism; their very experience of themselves and others is perfectionistic from the get-go. This is why efforts to undo perfectionism by an act of sheer will are hopeless. Commanding someone to stop being a perfectionist is like commanding an American who speaks only English to stop thinking in English. It simply cannot be done. Only someone who speaks multiple languages with some fluency can change their thinking from English to some other language, like German or Chinese. Similarly, only a person who is aware of and is somewhat fluent in alternative understandings of perfection has the freedom to think and feel non-perfectionistically. One purpose of this book is to teach you an alternative language of perfection so you can have the freedom to think, feel, and live non-perfectionistically, if you choose to do so. Whatever you choose, at least it will be a genuine choice for you once you have more than one language of perfection available to your mind.

The Schema of Flawlessness

Developmental, cognitive, and educational psychologists use the term *schema* to describe the cognitive process by which people come to think through a concept like perfectionism (Piaget, 1923; Bartlett, 1932; Anderson, 1998). A schema is a mental category. We have learned many, many schemas in our life spans, including schemas for trees, dogs, cars, houses, God, people, and everything in between. Some of these schemas have become so important to us and are often so powerfully reinforced by our culture that they become schematic, meaning they have become utterly fundamental to how we see ourselves and others. They color our experience of everything and everyone.

If a person becomes schematic for body weight, for example, then they will experience everyone they see in terms of some feature of their body type, be it skinny, obese, muscular, etc. They will evaluate themselves and others in terms of weight, and they will talk about weight-related matters almost all the time. Thinking through the cognitive category of body weight becomes characteristic of the person, a feature of their personality, as can be seen in people who suffer from certain eating disorders, for example. The same process occurs when someone becomes schematic for gender, race, intelligence, or socioeconomic status. They see and experience everything through the schema to which they have become attached.

We would suggest that many of us have become schematic for perfectionism. We think and feel in terms of flaws, failures, and errors, and we evaluate ourselves and others according to how well we are achieving flawlessness. Consequently, when we look at our faces in the mirror, we see our wrinkles, blemishes, and dark spots first and foremost. Indeed, that may be all we see. And we are jealous when other faces we see seem to be less flawed than our own. When we see a child misbehave, we think about how embarrassed the mother must be to have her child publicly reveal a fault in her parenting, and we may feel a little pride about our own parenting at the same time. When we look at a painting, even a masterpiece, our eyes seemingly automatically search for errors. And, as illustrated in chapter 1, when we give advice to other people who struggle with perfectionism, we can't help but talk about perfection in terms of flawlessness or being fully finished. We do not know why we evaluate everything in this perfectionistic way. It seems we have always done so, and it appears to be simply part of our nature as humans. Maybe we were just born this way.

That is not the case. Schemas, as the famous developmental theorist Jean Piaget taught, are developed. They are enculturated into our minds, but we do not have to become or remain schematic for any particular schema. Indeed, there are other cultures that do not value and reinforce perfectionism, and as a result, very few people in that culture are perfectionists. Similarly, there are people within our culture who are not schematic for perfectionism. They do not think through flawlessness at all, or at least they do so very little.

These differences across cultures and individuals within a culture suggest that we have agency in relation to our schemas. We can choose to be schematic or aschematic for any given cognitive category. However, the choice is often not an easy one to make, because perfectionism feels so natural and inevitable. It is our primary language. As such, we tend to take the schema for flawlessness for granted as the way things are or at least the way we are.

In order to change our minds, if we would choose to do so, we have to critically evaluate the schema of flawlessness and recognize it as a schema, not the way things are, and certainly not as the only way to conceive of perfection. To do that, we must understand where this schema originates and how it has been reinforced and habituated into our minds and our hearts. Then, once we understand how our language of perfectionism has become one and the same as our thoughts and feelings, we can begin to learn a different language, a new language, that will allow us to understand perfection differently and to think and feel differently about it, if we so desire.

A Brief Visit to Ancient Greece

As we stated in the first chapter, *perfection* is commonly defined as being free of faults or having the characteristic of flawlessness. But how did this definition of perfection come into being, and how did it gain such a strong hold on the Western mind? We will spare you all the details of the word's etymology here, but there are a few key points that need to be clarified. First, the ancient Greek philosophers who bequeathed to us the definition of *perfection* as flawlessness never intended for that definition to be applied to human beings. Human beings, after all, are physical creatures, and all physical things are capable of being changed, flawed, and defective.

Can you think of anything physical that can withstand change? Decay, erosion, disease, and death—nothing in this world escapes these imperfecting forces. Even the hardest and strongest physical substances we know of, like diamonds, can be cut, scratched, and even shattered. Human beings are certainly no exception to this rule. As part of the physical world, we are inevitably changeable and subject to flaws, as well.

The Metaphysical Realm of Flawlessness

The Greeks knew that flawlessness could not be found on this planet, so they conjured up another world, a metaphysical world (meaning literally "above or beyond the physical"), where the flawless ideals they could conceive of with their minds but could not find on earth could reside. Plato called this world the realm of ideal forms. It is here where everything, from a perfect form of a triangle to a perfect form of a person, could be found. These ideal forms, in order to be flawless, must be unchanging, unembodied, atemporal, and universal; in other words, completely unlike us.

Moreover, between this metaphysical realm and our own world lies an impassable divide. On one side of the divide are physical beings, like us, who can never be perfect, at least not in this life as embodied beings living in a world of flux. And on the other side of the divide are ideal forms, which can never be part of our world, for in the moment that an ideal form would enter our world, it would become subject to all of this world's imperfecting influences and its perfection would be destroyed. Thus, when it comes to human beings and flawlessness, never the twain shall meet.

Given this perspective, we can understand why so many people try to console perfectionists with the words, "nobody's perfect." They are simply pointing out something that Plato and other philosophers have known for centuries, which is that not one of us, as embodied beings in this physical world, can ever be truly flawless. No matter how hard we try and no matter how close we come, we will always fall short. Plato knew this would be the case, which is why he never intended the definition of perfection as flawlessness to be applied to human beings living in this world. And yet, somehow people like Katie (see chapter 1) feel upset and unworthy when they cannot achieve the impossible, when they cannot make themselves flawless. And they have convinced themselves that unless they achieve that faultless state of perfection here and now in this world of change, they can never be satisfied. They can never be at peace.

This was never Plato's plan for us. We will discuss his plan for us in a moment, but for now it is critically important to bear in mind that the concept of perfection that has become schematic for perfectionists, and for many of us who try to counsel and console them, is based on a false definition of the word perfection, as it relates to human beings. It is false because it was never intended to be applied to us. For the Greeks, who gave us this definition, it only applied to ideal forms in the metaphysical realm.

Imagining Perfection

A second key point that follows from the first and that also needs to be explicated here is the fact that although we cannot be flawless or create anything without fault in this world, we can imagine what an ideal form of ourselves or a thing would be. We can intuit flawlessness. Plato called this unique intuitive capacity of the human soul the "intellect." The intellect, he noted, allows our minds to make contact with the ideal forms in the metaphysical world through reason and imagination. For example, no mathematician can ever draw, carve, or even render a perfect triangle using a computer program, because that triangle will be part of our world and therefore subject to change and flaws. However, mathematicians can conceive of an ideal triangle in their minds. They can, for example, imagine the metaphysical triangle that is described by Pythagoras's theorem, $a^2 + b^2 = c^2$, as an ideal triangle that can never be erased, broken, or corrupted. Similarly, although not even Michelangelo can sculpt a flawless figure of the human form, as he may have attempted to do with his famous sculpture of the biblical figure David, he can still see in his mind's eye what a perfect human form could be in an ideal world.

The perfectionist, too, though she or he cannot live an error-free life, can imagine what life or even what one aspect of life would be like if he or she did not make any mistakes. You can do this, too. Think about it. Have you ever played a game, perhaps a simple game like checkers, and after losing you were immediately aware that there was a different, better game you should have played? If you let yourself dwell on it, you could see all the mistakes you made, and you would be simultaneously aware of the moves you should have made that would have led to success. When you did that, you were imagining the ideal form of your game. You were intuiting a sense of what could have been if you did not do anything wrong. For Plato, that was your intellect connecting to an ideal form of the game of checkers. The intellect for Plato is at the heart of learning and is the source of our understanding of the good, of truth, and of beauty. It connects us to metaphysical perfection. But this intellectual capacity, in the hands of a perfectionist, can develop into an unhealthy obsession rather than the healthy education Plato intended it to be.

Tantalized by the Fantasy of Flawlessness

The consequence of our intellect making contact with a world of ideal forms, coupled with our mistaken application of perfection defined as flawlessness to human beings, leads to a significant issue. Human beings are in the peculiar position of being able to imagine a flawless ideal that they deeply desire, but that will always elude their reach. We call this feature of perfectionism tantalization. The word *tantalize* originates in a Greek myth in which Tantalus, a mythological figure who behaved badly, was punished by the gods with a most horrific eternal form of suffering. He was chained in a pool of cool, fresh water, where the branches of a tree, heavy-laden with fruit, dangled above him in the air. As he reached for the fruit overhead, the branches would bend upward, keeping the fruit just out of his reach. And as he lowered his head or his hands toward the water to take a drink, the waters immediately receded so that he could not satisfy his thirst.

Tantalus was cursed to spend all eternity tormented by an unquenched hunger and thirst, with the fruit and the water that would satiate his desperate desires right there in front of his eyes, but always just barely beyond his grasp. So it is with perfectionism. The ideal version of you and of me that we yearn for is right there before us in our minds, yet it is always just out of our reach in our world of flux and flaws.

The Alternative of Perfection as Excellence

What are we to do with this state of affairs? For Plato, we ought not be tormented by the elusiveness of flawlessness because we were never meant to achieve it. We were meant only to model it or approximate it as best we can in our imperfect, physical world, knowing all the while that we would fall short of the ideal. For Plato, there is still a kind of perfection to be had in modeling or striving toward the ideal, but it is not a flawless perfection. Instead, it is a kind of excellence. Unlike flawless perfection, which does not come in degrees because it is complete and finished, excellence can be measured in terms of how closely our striving approximates an ideal standard in comparison with other models.

For example, Michael Phelps, arguably the greatest swimmer who has ever lived, is not and never could be a flawless swimmer, but he could be and clearly is an excellent swimmer. Indeed, he is arguably the most excellent swimmer. He is certainly a more excellent swimmer than any of us is. In his swimming there is something more essential, something truer of the ideal form of swimming than we would find in our own swimming, just as we find the essence of the ideal car more fully represented by a Ferrari than a Gremlin (just look up a picture of these cars and you will see what we mean). In that sense, Michael Phelps does approximate the ideal form more perfectly (i.e., more excellently) than we do, but he, too, can never achieve it.

Plato's plan for human beings, then, was not one of flawlessness. His was a plan of excellence. We ought to be as excellent as possible in our thinking, feeling, and behaving, knowing that we will err and fail in our efforts. Failures are to be expected and ought not to cause us despair, for we live in an imperfect world as imperfect beings. For Plato, we can and should only do the best we can to model the ideal, and those who do it better than others ought to be rewarded and empowered for their superior excellence (e.g., philosopher-kings). Those who do it worse need further education and more opportunities for growth.

Christianity's Contribution

Despite Plato's best intentions and the obvious logical and practical impossibilities entailed in applying the flawless conception of perfection to human beings, flawlessness, not excellence has become the standard for human perfection. This is due in large part to Christianity. Specifically, Christ's commandment that we must be perfect even as our Father who is in heaven is perfect was interpreted to mean that we must be as God is. Because God is assumed to be flawless, He must dwell in the metaphysical realm (i.e. heaven), and His perfection could not be merely excellence. He must also be ideal, unchanging, and without defect.

To be as our heavenly Father is, we, too, would have to be not only excellent but also flawless and without fault, even as physical beings living in a physical world. In other words, we must do the impossible if we are to keep Christ's commandment to be perfect. We will show in greater detail in the next chapter that neither flawlessness nor excellence are intended by that commandment, but for now, consider the consequences of making the impossible feature of flawlessness the criterion of human perfection.

First, the Christian perfectionist believes that in order to be perfect as God is perfect, he or she must be flawless. Second, using the intellect, the perfectionist can imagine what a flawless version of him- or herself would be and do. Third, the Christian perfectionist is tantalized and tormented by the ideal form of him- or herself, which he or she is commanded by Christ to be, but which always lies just beyond his or her grasp. Fourth, as a kind of consolation prize for falling short of flawlessness, the perfectionist can at least take pride in approximating flawlessness more excellently than other people. The result of that "prize" for Christians is often a paradoxical mix of self-loathing for not keeping God's commandment, and self-righteousness for pulling it off better than others. Does that sound about right? Can you think of anyone who fits this description?

For us, the people known in the New Testament as the scribes and the Pharisees come to mind as a prime example of people who are schematic in this perfectionistic way. These men "shut up the kingdom of heaven against men" (Matthew 23:13), including those who are "entering to go in," and even themselves. Why did they shut everyone out of heaven? Because they knew it would be impossible for any person to keep the Law flawlessly, and they believed flawlessness was the price of admission to heaven. Undoubtedly, the scribes and Pharisees used their intellect to imagine the ideal of a flawless Law-abider, for this was the standard they used in judging others, including Christ.

These men were clearly also tantalized by the ideal of flawlessness. Consistent with being schematic, flawlessness before the Law became all they could think about. They judged themselves and everyone else according to how well they kept the Law, so much so that they were blind to the perfect Being, the Law-giver Himself who walked among them. Instead of worshiping Him, they wanted Him dead because He had claimed to have achieved what so clearly eluded all of them. Finally, if heaven was shut to them for their lack of flawlessness, they appeared to find at least some solace in endeavoring to be more excellent in keeping the Law than all others. Indeed, they fancied themselves to be the most excellently righteous persons in all of Judea, even though they knew that would not be enough to get them into heaven. Unfortunately, if they were excellent at anything at all, it was in being judgmental and self-righteous, not in the practice of true piety and devotion to their God. But such things are inevitable when the fantasy of flawlessness is in play.

Perfectionism's Emotional Engine

The schema of perfectionism's grip on our mind can be very strong, but it is its hold upon our hearts that has led it to be the primary, if not the only language of perfection that we speak. And how has it gotten hold of our hearts so strongly? Well, it is really quite simple: When we make a mistake, when we fail, when we do something wrong, it hurts. It hurts us, and even worse, it often hurts someone else, frequently someone whom we care for deeply. When that happens, when our misdoings injure another person, it is almost too much for us to bear. We become filled with regret, and we wish we could magically do something to undo our error.

If We Could Turn Back Time

If only we could be like Superman, as played by Christopher Reeve, in the final scenes of the 1978 movie of the same name. In those scenes, Superman is trying to save everyone's lives during a horrible earthquake caused by his arch nemesis, Lex Luthor. But even with his super speed, he cannot be everywhere at the same time, for he, too, is part of the physical world and therefore flawed, even if he is more excellent than the rest of us. In all of his efforts to save everyone, he forgets to save the person he cares about most in the world, Lois Lane. She dies in the earthquake as her car is swallowed up by the earth; she suffocates beneath the dirt that engulfs her.

Superman arrives just a hair too late, pulls the car out of the ground, rips off the door, and pulls her out. She is already dead. Despite all his superpowers, he was not fast enough. He was not perfect. He lets out a superhuman scream of anguish, and then, against the laws of nature and the will of his Kryptonian father, Jor-El, he uses his powers to reverse the rotation of the earth and turn back time so he can make things right, so he can rescue Lois. Oh, if only we, too, could turn back time! If only we could make right what our sins and mistakes have made so very wrong! If we cannot live a flawless life, can we at least reverse time and make our errors right?

Of course, we are not Superman and we cannot turn back time. Our failures and mistakes remain part of our permanent life record and haunt us forever in the form of our memories of past events. I recall when I was young, more than one perfection- ist-minded church teacher stating that after this life, when we are judged by God, all of our past actions, thoughts, and feelings will be presented like a movie on a large screen for everyone to see. Nothing will be left out. Every flaw, every sin, every mistake will be displayed in full clarity. The thought of this movie premier was horrifying to me. Even as a young person hearing this, I had already made so many mistakes and committed so many sins, many of which were painfully embarrassing, and all of which I hoped no one ever noticed or remembered. The idea of my mom and dad, siblings and friends, and God Himself sitting in the audience to view a movie of my flaw-ridden life was just about the scariest thing I could imagine. It would hurt them all so badly to see how I had let them down, and that would destroy me!

I don't know what my teachers intended when they shared this metaphor, but the thought of this horrifying display of all my sins and failings did not heighten my awareness of my dependency on Christ's mercy and grace. It did not incline me toward repentance. It provided one clear unmistakable message: "Don't make any more mistakes than you have already. Do everything right from now on and you won't have to fear what else will be in your movie. You won't have to live with any more regret than you already have. You won't further disappoint your parents and your God. Just be perfect from now on, all the time, and you will have nothing more to worry about when the day of your judgment comes."

Controlled by Our Fear of Regret

To avoid regret and shame, perfectionists can literally make themselves crazy. One woman's fear of making mistakes that would lead to regret became so strong after the birth of her son that she developed a severe, debilitating obsessive-compulsive disorder. For example, whenever she drove with her son to the store and would come upon a stop sign or a red light along the way, she would have to turn and look at him in his car seat. She could not take her eyes off of him until she began to accelerate, for fear that while she was stopped someone might snatch her child or inject him with an infected needle or otherwise injure him. On the rare occasion that she took her son for a walk in the stroller, she had to make sure the stroller wheels didn't touch any cigarette butts on the ground and she had to steer clear of passersby, fearing that human saliva, human breath, or any other physical contact would infect the child in some way and make him ill or even kill him.

At home, she had to wash her hands almost every minute so that she didn't infect the baby herself. Everything had to be clean and spotless inside the house. Each day she would scrub down the entire house with antibacterial wipes. She felt she had to protect her son from every germ. Her house was immaculate, not because she wanted to show it off, but because she lived in constant fear of making a mistake. If she let her guard down, even for a moment, she might allow the most horrific of illnesses to afflict her baby.

This poor woman believed she had to be flawless or her greatest fears for her son would be realized, and if they were realized it would be her fault and she would not be able to live with that horrible regret and guilt. Thus, she was compelled to repeat certain behaviors incessantly in a futile attempt to control herself, her environment, and her child so that her deepest fears would not come to fruition. This is not vanity. This is not a concern with looking like she had everything together. This was sheer horror at the thought of doing anything wrong that might result in an injury to her infant, and it is this horror, this fear that beats in the heart of perfectionists.

This young mother would be the first person to tell you that she knows that what she is doing is not healthy. She even knows that her compulsions are having a negative impact on her son. She realizes that in actuality her disorder is the greatest threat to his well-being, but she still cannot stop herself. Her feet start walking toward the kitchen sink to wash her hands automatically, and she cannot will herself to stop them. Her thinking, her behaviors, her relationships with her husband, her son, and other people, are all made unhealthy by her OCD, and it breaks her heart, but she is helpless before her disorder because the specter of regret at the idea of a failure that would result in her son suffering in any way completely hijacks her and holds all other motivations hostage. And she can see no way out of this morass because she knows only one language of perfection, the language of flawlessness, and if she could only be flawless, then there would be no regret.

We can all relate, at some level, to this suffering mother. Each of us has made mistakes, committed sins, and erred in ways that caused someone else to suffer, including in many cases, someone who was innocent, and each of us feels the weight of the suffering we have caused others resting squarely upon our shoulders. Like Adam and Eve, whose transgression brought all future people into a lone and dreary world, our mistakes and the injuries they cause others are our own fall from Eden. And in the painful, awful wake of that fall, we cannot help but think, "If only I had taken a taxi that night when I drank a little more than I should have, I would not have hit that car and disabled that teenage girl." "If only I had visited my friend who I knew was depressed and needed help, I could have gotten him the help he needed and he would not have committed suicide." "If only I had not said those hurtful things to my teenage daughter, she would not have run away." "If only I had not hit my wife in the heat of that argument, she would not have left me." If only...if only...if only.

Whether the offense was large or small, whether it hurt one person or many, we have all offended someone and broken a heart at some point, if not at many points, in our lives, and we all know that the injury we caused could have been avoided if we had acted differently, if we had acted flawlessly. Or if the injury could not be avoided, then, at least, if our actions had been flawless, we would be blameless in the situation. We also know that once the mistake is committed and the damage is done, we can never go back and undo it. It is a permanent part of our past. We must live forever with the consequences of our errors and flaws, including the increased suffering we have caused.

This, for the perfectionist, is the greatest suffering of all. This is the suffering we simply cannot bear. To have injured an innocent, or even a not-so-innocent, other, whether by an intentional or an unintentional mistake, is the worst of all possible sins. It feels unforgivable. We don't know whether we even want to be forgiven for it, because it is so bad, so wrong, and so permanent.

Conclusion

The language of perfectionism, as you can see, is a matter of both the mind and the heart. The mind conceives of the ideal and holds the perfectionist and those around him or her accountable to its impossible standard, while the heart desperately yearns to achieve the ideal so as not to hurt others or suffer the pain of regret. When flawlessness tantalizes us in this way, the mind tries to console the heart with the pursuit of excellence and a favorable comparison to others, but excellence will work only until a mistake is made and someone suffers for it—and mistakes are always made and someone always suffers. Flawlessness alone can satisfy the perfectionist's mind and heart, so it becomes the only language of perfection that the perfectionist knows.

CHAPTER 3

"Be Ye Therefore Perfect!"

Imperfection is the wound that lets God in.

—*Kurtz & Ketcham*

The first step we must take in learning a new language of perfection is gaining a proper understanding of the commandment to "be ye therefore perfect, even as your father which is in heaven is perfect" (Matthew 5:48 kjv). As we have demonstrated, this commandment lies dead-center at the heart of the paradox of perfectionism. If this verse of Scripture is interpreted as a command to be without fault or flaw, then the paradox of perfectionism and all the features associated with it are inevitable, and could even be interpreted as being God's will. Of course, this makes Christ's commandment to be perfect, when interpreted as "be flawless," an even stranger commandment than we have already shown it to be, because it contradicts Christ's other commandments to repent and come unto Him (Matthew 11:28; John 7:37; Mark 1:15). As we pointed out, if we could somehow keep the command to be flawless, we would have no sins for which we would need to come unto Christ and be redeemed. Our flawlessness would negate the need to depend on His grace and mercy.

It is hard to imagine that contradicting commandments, choices between blamelessness and Christ, and frustration at never achieving an always elusive ideal are part of God's plan for us. If we are going to have to live under such circumstances and accept the possibility that such confusion, frustration, and suffering are God's will for us, we had better make sure, to the extent we are able, that we properly understand perfection as Christ commanded it. In order to understand that commandment properly, we invite you to consider that the answer to the seemingly impossible conundrum of perfectionism depends on the way in which the perfection of God is understood and upon the definition of perfection the Lord intended when He issued the command.

The Perfection Christ Commands of Us

To properly understand the form of perfection Christ intended when He issued the command in Matthew 5:48, we have to look at that commandment in the broader context of the verses that accompany it. Including the surrounding verses would seem to be especially important in this instance, because Christ commanded His disciples to "be ye *therefore* perfect" (emphasis ours). The word *therefore* clearly refers the disciples back to the description of perfection that Christ gave earlier in His teaching on the topic. Indeed, the kind of perfection the Savior was interested in His disciples emulating and obeying in verse 48 had already been described to them in the previous verses. And what kind of perfection did the Lord describe?

In verses 43–47, we learn that the form of God's perfection that we are commanded to obey in this life is the perfection of God's love. And how is God's love perfect? As these verses show, God's love is perfect because it is completely inclusive and whole. That is, He loves both those who love Him and those who do not, both His friends and His enemies. No one escapes His love. It circumscribes all of His children.

Not only that, but He also blesses all of His children, including the just and the unjust, with His sunshine and His rain, because He loves them all evenly and is no respecter of persons in that regard. In this sense, God's love is perfect because it is complete, but it is also perfect because it is even and level across all of His children. He does not tip the scales of His love or the blessings that ensue from His love in favor of any group or individual, even if they are more just and good. When it comes to God's love, no one stands above or below another.

This indicates that the Lord's command to us in Matthew 5:48 is not to be sinless and without flaw, which as we have already shown is impossible and was never intended to apply to human beings. Rather, we are commanded to love completely and even- ly, meaning to love all people, our friends and our enemies, the same. We recognize that the commandment to love both friend and enemy may still seem impossible to you, but as we will show in the chapters that follow, that is not necessarily the case. At the very least, loving as our God loves us is surely not a logical impossibility, as would be flawlessness for inescapably flawed beings. It is also not practically impossible. On the contrary, it is possible to love fully and evenly, even if only briefly, as we are filled with the love of God. We can do this as flawed and sinful beings, because it is not our love, but the love of God in us that is perfect.

Moreover, because this form of perfection consists of love and not sinlessness, we can repent when our love is incomplete and unbalanced, and through the grace and mercy of the Lord and Savior, we can be filled with His perfect love again and genu- inely obey His commandment to be perfect, even as our Father in heaven is perfect. Perhaps you can even remember a time, or maybe even multiple times, when you have repented and in God's forgiving grace you have been filled with His love for all people. These moments of whole and complete love may be more rare and brief in duration than we would like, but they offer sufficient evidence that it is possible to keep the commandment to be perfect in this life, if only for a short time, and your personal experiences of God's love confirm that you have already done so. If you do not believe you have yet experienced God's love, then stick with us and keep reading, and see if you can begin, ever so incrementally, to learn this language of His perfect love.

The Paradox of Christ

If the perfection commanded of us is to love as God loves, wholly and evenly, then we are in no way capable of that kind of perfection by ourselves. Human love is partial, contingent, and imbalanced. We love some people more than others, and we find it difficult to love people who do not love us or do not seem to love anyone. We have all thought we knew what love was at one point in life, only to realize later that the way we felt at that time was not really love at all. We have fallen in love and out of love, and we have discovered that different people mean very different things by the word love. Even a physically abusive husband and father claims to love his victimized wife and children.

Some of the people who study love write of different love languages, different forms or types of love, and varied styles of love. But these same researchers also admit that they are very much at a loss when it comes to truly *understanding* love. As one president of the American Psychological Association put it, "So far as love or affection is concerned, psychologists have failed in this mission. The little we know about love does not transcend simple observation, and the little we write about it has been written better by poets and novelists" (Harlow, 1958, 673). To put all of this confusion around the idea of love in terms that the perfectionist understands, we would say that human love is flawed and prone to error, and that our efforts to understand it constitute a history that is full of mistakes and failures.

God surely knows this all too well. Like all characteristics of human beings, who are fallen and sinful, so, too, is our love. That is why He gave us His only begotten Son, who offered Himself as a sacrifice for sin, so that we might not only be redeemed by Him, but also so that we might love with His love, with godly love. But how is this possible? Is not godly love metaphysical love, and therefore unchanging, unembodied, flawless, and atemporal? How can we as physical beings ever achieve such a love? Isn't godly love an ideal that can only tantalize us and remain always just beyond our reach?

Fully God, Fully Human

We would answer these questions affirmatively were it not for the paradox of Christ, His godly form being flawless and without blemish, who willingly, according to the Christian existentialist Soren Kierkegaard (1991), "abased" himself for our sakes, taking upon himself the human form, and not only the human form, but the human form of an infant, the most dependent, fragile, and vulnerable of all creatures. By doing so, He subjected Himself to all the flaws and imperfecting effects of the physical world in which we live.

If Christ's mother were to have dropped Him, He would have been bruised ("for our iniquities", Isaiah 53:5). If, as a young carpenter's apprentice, Christ had cut Himself while learning to saw wood with His father, then He would have been left with a scar. The very fact that He bore the wounds of the crucifixion on His hands and feet, even as a resurrected being, shows that He allowed Himself to be changed by the world He inhabited. More than that, He had to learn to walk, to speak, and to read. He allowed Himself to be flawed, incomplete, and dependent upon others. He subjected Himself to the processes of physical, cognitive, emotional, and spiritual development. He was, by all Platonic accounts, an imperfect being.

And yet He committed no sin. He was pure and holy, working miracles, teaching parables, and resurrecting Himself on the third day after His crucifixion. He lived a perfect life, flawless in His character, blameless in His righteousness, and faultless in His treatment of others. He was, in other words, fully human and fully divine, capable of experiencing all the imperfecting effects of our world while also living a sinless life. In this sense, Christ is truly a paradox.

A God of Weakness

But the paradox of Christ goes deeper still. The paradox of Christ includes the fact that His divine nature gave Him unlimited power and yet He chose to embrace and emulate weakness in His walk of life. He did not come into the world riding a chariot of fire and lay waste to the nonbeliever and the hypocrite alike with His blazing sword of justice. He did not compel or control the minds and hearts of people. He did not practice the forms of power that the people of His time expected from a god. Instead, He grew up poor, was essentially homeless during His ministry, "and there [was] no beauty that we should desire him" (Isaiah 53:2).

Even after fasting in the wilderness for forty days and nights—which was likely the duration of time required for Christ to weaken Himself to the point that He could have experienced temptation just as we do, as weak, fragile, fully human beings— He did not give in to the temptations of the devil, all of which were temptations to power: power over nature (turning stones into bread), power over heaven (calling angels from heaven to protect Him from crashing to the ground), and power over people (ruling over the kingdoms of the world). As starved, exhausted, and worn out as He must have been, He still rejected these temptations to power. Instead, as Kierkegaard put it, He maintained His abasement, willingly remaining weak, poor, and destitute for our sakes. This is the true paradox of Christ and the heart of the Christian miracle: a God, capable of the greatest power, withholds that power and chooses instead weakness, frailty, and poverty.

Why would He do that? Why would He willingly choose weakness? We find a key to this paradox in Paul's letter to the Hebrews:

> For verily he took not on him the nature of angels; but he took on him the seed of Abraham. Wherefore in all things it behooved him to be made like unto his brethren, that he might be a merciful and faithful high priest in things pertaining to God, to make reconciliation for the sins of the people. For in that he himself hath suffered being tempted, he is able to succor them that are tempted (Hebrews 2:16–18).

Christ chose "to be made like unto" us so that He could be merciful toward us, so He could make reconciliation for our sins, and so He could succor us. He embraced His full humanity so He could know us fully in our humanity—Indeed, in order to know and succor each of us, even the weakest, poorest, and most destitute of us, He chose to be made like the weakest, poorest, and most destitute of us. In this way, no person is beyond His reach, no one escapes His empathy or His compassion. He is truly a God "among us" (John 1:14).

And what motivates the paradox of Christ, His submission to weakness, poverty, and destitution? Recall that in Matthew 5:43–48, Christ commanded His disciples to be perfect, even as their Father in heaven was perfect, meaning that we must love as God loves—wholly, completely, and evenly. Christ makes Himself like unto the least among us, because He loves all of us without exception, not just one group or individual. It is not just a love of the part, but it is a love of the whole. It is not a love that runs out or runs short; it is complete. It is not imbalanced toward any person or group, no matter how righteous or wicked they may be. Thus, He condescended Himself below all of us, so that His love can encompass the whole of humanity and so that His mercy and succoring is complete and all-reaching. It is a total love, a perfect love.

Perfect Love in an Imperfect World

Christ's love is also whole, in that He bridged the gap between human and godly love by embodying divine love as a human being living in the physical world. In other words, because He was fully divine and fully human, He alone could love perfectly as God does, but He could also do that as one of us, even as the weakest and lowliest among us. By doing so, Christ literally and personally made Himself the bridge between the metaphysical and the physical, if you prefer the Greek terminology, or in Christian terms, He made Himself an intercessory between our Father, who is in heaven, and us here on earth. As a result, if we come unto Him who is accessible to us in His humanity, as one of us, then we also come into contact with His divinity, and with His perfect and godly love. Thus, as we accept the embrace of His grace and mercy, which is at once a fully human and fully divine embrace, He makes us capable of loving as He loves, which is to love as our Father in heaven loves, enabling us to obey His commandment to be therefore perfect even as our Father, who is in heaven, is perfect.

This is why John wrote, "We love him, because he first loved us" (1 John 4:19). We depend on the love of God bestowed upon us by our personal relationship to Christ for our capacity to love God and our fellow human beings. Christ must love us first, because He alone can bring divine love into the human world. Thus, we can only love wholly, completely, and evenly after the love of God fills us up, and that love comes only from our Savior, rather than from some self-generated counterfeit of God's love.

Paul makes this point crystal clear in 1 Corinthians 13. Without charity, the perfect love of Christ, Paul's love is merely human love. It is as a "sounding brass, or a tinkling cymbal" (verse 1). If he does not have charity, he "is nothing" and his actions, as good and noble as they may be, are of no profit to him. Absent charity, prophecies will fail, tongues will cease, and knowledge will vanish. This is because prophecies, knowledge, and love, without God's love infusing them, are only partial. They are not whole and complete unless and until "that which is perfect is come, then that which is in part shall be done away" (verse 10). When charity, or the pure love of God comes, all is made whole and our actions will be fueled by divine love, a love that includes all people and is not "puffed up" (verse 4) above them. Perhaps it is for this reason that Paul wrote in his letter to the Colossians that "above all these things put on charity, which is the bond of perfectness" (3:14).

Glory in Weakness

How is it that we can "put on charity"? How can we be filled with the love of Christ? How can we love perfectly? First, we must overcome our perfectionistic disdain for weakness. Paul himself struggled with this challenge. As someone who, like other Pharisees, had been empowered by his blamelessness before the Law for most of his life, embracing weakness for Christ's sake was not always easy. In the twelfth chapter of his second epistle to the Corinthians, for example, Paul acknowledges his own resistance to weakness. He writes that when he was given "a thorn in the flesh" (verse 7) to "buffet" him, he "besought the Lord thrice, that it might depart from me" (verse 8). Paul wanted to be free of this weakening agent, even if the thorn in his flesh served the purpose of ensuring that he would not "be exalted above measure" (verse 7). The response of the Lord, however, showed Paul a better way, even the Lord's way, to understand his weakness. The Lord said unto Paul, "My grace is sufficient for thee: *for my strength is made perfect in weakness*" (verse 9).

Two very important teachings are made manifest in these words. First, Christ's grace is sufficient for Paul, as it is for all of us. But in what sense is it sufficient? Most people think of it being sufficient for salvation, which is true. We are not saved based on our own merits; we are saved based upon the merits of Christ. But, for the purposes of this book, and for the purposes of our discussion on perfection, consider that the Lord's grace is also sufficient for perfection, for it is only by His grace that we can love wholly and completely; it is only by His grace and mercy that we can put on charity. His grace is sufficient for us to love as He loves.

The second important teaching is that Christ's strength is made perfect—that is, His love is made whole, complete, and accessible to us—in weakness. We have already noted that by making Himself literally a god "among us," rather than a god above us or beyond us, Christ embodied and manifested the love of God, as one of us, even the least among us. By doing so, He made it possible for us to be succored by Him and to love with His love, the love of God. He bridged, or made whole, divine and human love within Himself and He did it in a state of utter weakness and indigence. As a result, His love encompasses all of humankind and circumscribes heaven and earth within its reach. Nothing escapes the love of Jesus Christ. His strength, which is His love, is whole and complete: in a word, perfect.

Now, understanding and appreciating the Lord's way, Paul writes, "Most gladly therefore will I rather glory in my infirmities, that the power of Christ may rest upon me. Therefore I take pleasure in infirmities, in reproaches, in necessities, in persecutions, in distresses for Christ's sake: *for when I am weak, then am I strong*" (2 Corinthians 12:9–10, emphasis ours). Rather than despise his weakness, however it may have come upon him, Paul learns to glory in weakness, because in his infirmities, the power of Christ can and will rest upon him. In other words, if he is meek, humble, and lowly of heart, as is Christ, then he will be filled with charity and he will be perfected in Christ. He will be made strong, but not as a Pharisee is strong in his blamelessness before the Law, but strong as a disciple of Christ, whose love is

THE PARADOX OF PERFECTION • 49

his strength, even as he stands blameworthy before Christ as a fallen, flawed, and sinful being.

It was likely not easy for Paul, who as a Pharisee was blameless before the Law, to learn this lesson, and it certainly is not easy for us who have become schematic for perfectionism to learn to glory in weakness. Indeed, the thought of glorying in our weakness seems wholly backward and absurd. Most of us have been taught to look at weakness as being akin to a virus. We ought to avoid it if we can, but if we do somehow get infected by it, we must do whatever it takes to get rid of it. The only good thing about a virus is that once it passes through us, we will have developed antibodies to it so that we will never again suffer its effects upon us. From the perspective of this virus model, then, we ultimately can overcome our weaknesses and become strong.

While this conception of a virus may be usefully applied to matters of physical health, it is not a proper analogy for spiritual health and well-being. Sin does make us spiritually weak and sick, as does adversity, infirmity, and injury by others, but these things are not viruses that need to be avoided or purged from our souls. Instead, they are the very things that allow the physician, Christ, to heal us with His forgiveness. Speaking of Himself as the physician, Christ taught in Mark 2:17 that "they that are whole have no need of the physician, but they that are sick." Were we without spiritual sickness, without weakness and frailty, we would not need to be healed, and we would not need Christ. He could do nothing for us. But because we are spiritually sick and flawed and in need of the Healer's miraculous mercy, He can come to us and offer us His love, His forgiveness, and His grace.

Once healed by Christ's forgiveness, we do not develop an immunity to sin. We will sin and err again, but that is to be expected of fallen human beings, and it is desirable, not because sin and error, or infirmities and persecution, are desirable things in and of themselves. No one should pursue sin, sickness, or persecution for their own sakes, but these things will happen nevertheless. And because they are inevitable, these weaknesses make us constantly dependent upon the Savior's mercy, grace, and love. They keep us wholly reliant upon repentance and the healing forgiveness that only Christ can provide, and because they bind us to our Lord, they are, in that sense, desirable.

It is our weakness, then, that enables perfection, not our flawlessness or strength. By hating our weakness, we actually deny Christ access to our hearts. In this sense, Christian perfection has its own paradox: You must be imperfect for Christ to perfect you. It is for this reason that we, like Paul, ought to be "glad, when we are weak" (2 Corinthians 12:9).

Leveling

The paradox of Christ enables our perfection (i.e., our loving as God loves) because He has made Himself even with us, allowing us to love as He loves, even as the Father loves. He does not reach His hand toward us from the heavens above, like Michelangelo's God reaching toward Adam from the metaphysical realm, nor does He expect us to erect towers, like the tower of Babel, that will raise us up to Him. Instead, Christ willingly came down to our level to be yoked with us as one of us.

Yokes are an important symbol for our relationship to Christ and His leveling or evenness with us. A yoke, which is usually made of wood and possibly iron, was placed over the necks of two animals, such as oxen, who were then hitched to wagons, carts, or plows to work together in unison to more efficiently transport loads or plow fields. As the animals work together under the yoke, the shared burden is made lighter on both of them. The more intimately the animals understand each other, the more effectively the animals will work together and the easier it will be to pull the load. The yoke then suggests two meanings. First, it connotes servitude. The animals pulling the yoke serve the wagon driver or the farmer plowing the field as they are placed under his or her yoke. Second, the yoke indicates teamwork. The animals work together under the yoke as a unified pair to more effectively complete the task.

When Christ invites us to take His yoke upon us, He is speaking as our master and asks us to become His servants. He promises us that if we submit ourselves to Him, He will provide us with an easy yoke and a light burden to carry. At the same time, He speaks to us as a fellow yoke bearer, as a servant. He has willingly submitted Himself to His own yoke and has subjected Himself to the will of His Father, accepting the burden of humanity and giving Himself over to the work of our salvation. Thus, He calls out to us to be yoked with Him as fellow servants of the Father, even as He is also our Master. In this way, He joins us in the muck and the mire, allowing Himself to be dirtied, just as we are, and He does it for our sakes. Thus, He is the quintessential servant-leader.

He shares the yoke with us so that we can take part in pulling His burden, which is light. It is light, in part, because He brings no burdens of His own sin or infirmity to the task, for He is sinless and fully divine. The only burden He brings to our work is the burden of His love. If we take upon us His yoke, then we have access to His love, but in receiving that love we also have to be willing to carry His love into the world, for He commands us to love one another as He loves us. His yoke is also easy because He will not slacken nor become weary in loving us and the world. He will pull hard and true, even if we tire or grow faint, even if we fail to love as He loves, and because of His constancy in loving us, our part in the labor of His love will always be easy and light.

The Rules of the Yoke

Anyone who uses a yoke knows that there are a few rules that must be followed if the two animals under the yoke are going to work well together. First, the yoke only works if the animals are side by side. The yoke will not work if one animal is ahead of or behind the other, or if one animal is above or below the other. They must be right next to each other pulling together on an even plane. Second, yokes are ineffective if the two animals yoked together are not alike. For example, if one animal is an ox and the other a mule, even though both are beasts of burden, they will not be able to work well as a team because of their different breeds, sizes, strides, temperaments, etc. Finally, the pair will not pull effectively if both animals assume a dominant role. One must lead and the other must fall in line as the follower. If both animals try to take the lead in the pairing, the work will go nowhere. One of the animals must submit to the other.

All three of these rules apply to the yoke of Christ. First, Christ placed Himself right alongside humankind, allowing Himself to grow and develop from a baby to a child to a teenager to an adult, just as we do. He did not skip any steps or arrive in a fully developed state. He lived as we live and experienced what we experience in each of the developmental stages of our lives. In this sense, He does not walk ahead of us or behind us, above us or below us. Yoked to us, He walks at our pace and at our level.

Second, Christ did not come to earth as an angel or some other heavenly being. He came to this world as one of us, as a person, a human being, so that He could be like us and so that He could succor us. Because we are of the same "breed," He knows exactly what it is like to feel, think, and behave as we do. He understands us fully and knows exactly how to work alongside us.

Finally, Christ will not compel us to take up His yoke, nor will He force us to submit to His will once we are yoked to Him, but He does invite us to follow Him, to submit to His will and let Him guide our shared work and our shared life. If we resist that submission, if we assert our dominance, the yoke will not function as it should, the task will become hard, the burden will feel heavy, and we will not make progress.

A Telling Illustration

The metaphor of our relationship with Christ being like a yoke is powerfully illustrated throughout the Old and New Testaments of the Bible. The example of Christ's actions when a woman who had been caught in adultery by the Pharisees was brought before Him for judgment is particularly indicative of Christ's invitation for us to take His yoke upon us and His willingness to make Himself even with us as one of us in that endeavor.

Recall that the Pharisees and scribes brought the adulteress before Jesus, who was sitting and teaching people in the temple. They set her in the midst of them and then sought to tempt Jesus to judge her, stating that the Law demanded that she be stoned for her sin. One can imagine what her experience must have been like. She had been caught in the very act of adultery. There was no chance that she would be found innocent, as she was clearly guilty. She must have known the punishment for her transgression was death by stoning, and that must have frightened her and made her feel hopeless about any sort of mercy or compassion coming her way. Her death was imminent, and she knew it.

But Jesus did not take the Pharisees' bait, and He did not act as they expected Him to. Instead, He stooped down, down to her level, and He wrote on the ground with His finger, acting as though He did not even hear them. The message of His body language here is so clear: He lowered himself to the level of the adulteress, beneath the high and haughty stance of the Pharisees and Scribes, and below the elevated position that God on earth had every right to maintain. He stooped down and He abased Himself, and by so doing put Himself right alongside this woman who was completely guilty and fully sinful as someone who had just committed one of the most grievous sins under the Law.

Failing to appreciate the momentous significance of Christ's nonverbal communication, the woman's accusers continued to press Christ for a judgment, hoping to entrap Him. Eventually, Christ stood up and met the Pharisees' eyes with His own, on their level, the level they pretended to occupy, the level of blamelessness before the Law, a level He alone could achieve. The words He then spoke to them, typically read as an indictment, were actually an important invitation to the Pharisees and scribes: "He that is without sin among you, let him first cast a stone at her" (John 8:7). He then stooped back down and wrote again on the ground. His verbal and nonverbal invitation to the Pharisees and scribes was simple: "Be honest with yourselves. Acknowledge your own sinfulness and come down from your proud, pretended stance to join Me and this woman down here. For down here where this woman is, this is the place where we all truly are, and it is here where I, Christ, have willingly placed Myself so that I can succor you and share My yoke with you." Surely, He knew none of them would accept His invitation, but it is just as sure that if one or more of them had accepted it, He would have happily embraced them.

Again, blinded to Christ's message by their own perfectionism, they all left, one by one, receiving Christ's words more as an indictment than an invitation and feeling "convicted by their own conscience" (verse 9). After they all departed, only the woman was left with Christ alongside her. How interesting it is that the sinner alone is left with the Lord. Where else could Christ be? The Pharisees and scribes rejected Him for they had no need of Him, or so they thought. They had the Law, so they needed no yoke and no Savior. Their answer to the question we asked in chapter 1 was very clear. They wanted flawlessness and blamelessness, not Christ.

The sinner, on the other hand, likely still looking to the ground and still fearing the inevitable stoning that she believed surely awaited her, might not have noticed Christ's face, on an even level with hers, as He gently inquired, "Woman, where are those thine accusers?" (verse 10). Lifting her eyes just enough to see who remained to stone her, she noted, probably to her own surprise, that "no man" (verse 11) remained. There were no accusers, for the only One who was able to remain, the only One who was without sin, the only One who had every right to cast the first stone at the woman, had no desire to do so. Instead, filled with mercy and compassion, the Savior uttered words that must have salved the woman's broken heart like a healing balm: "Neither do I condemn thee: go and sin no more" (verse 11).

Now, lifted by Christ's forgiveness and kindness, the woman stood as Christ stood with her, raised from her lowly and sinful place to walk in the light of His love, fully upright and without fear of condemnation. Unlike the Pharisees and the scribes, she accepted His invitation, and she came unto Him and took His yoke upon her. The load became easy and the burden became light. She, too, answered the question from chapter 1, and her answer is very clear: "I choose you, Lord, my Savior and Redeemer." Can anyone doubt that she was filled with the love of God? Can anyone deny that this love emanated from her countenance and her whole being and that she loved all people in that moment?

We don't know the rest of this woman's story, but it is hard to imagine that she left Christ feeling anything but His love, wholly and completely. And if she carried that love with her as she departed, then by doing so she kept the commandment to be perfect, even as her Father in heaven is perfect. It is impossible to imagine a perfect adulteress given the language of perfectionism, but in terms of the language of perfect love, that is exactly what she was in that moment.

Christ makes possible this same perfection for each one of us who chooses Him over flawlessness. By condescending below all things, that is by making Himself weak, like unto the least of us, Christ has made Himself capable of meeting every person at every level of sin, despair, and hopelessness. By making Himself even with us, He can succor us in our darkest hour and lift us up from the depths that would otherwise imprison us. This is the chief and most marvelous manifestation of His love: He weakens

Himself in order to meet us where we are, extends His yoke to us, and then makes our burdens light.

He does the same thing for us when we are proud and arrogant. He invites us to come down from our self-erected pedestal and be with Him. Consider, for example, His parable in Luke 14, where He teaches that if we are invited to a wedding, we should not seat ourselves in the upper chambers, lest the host and the groom come to us and move us to the lower rooms to make room for those more honorable and deserving than we are. No, we should voluntarily seat ourselves in the lower chambers. Then, if the host and groom happen to come to us and invite us to sit in the upper room, we are welcome to go there.

The Pharisees and scribes, like each of us when we become lifted up in pride, have seated themselves above others, as if they were in heaven already. As happened with the woman caught in adultery, Christ showed them easily with His body language that they were in the wrong place, in the wrong state of mind, and He invited them to join Him and the woman in the low and proper place where we all are as flawed and sinful beings. Surely, if they had accepted His invitation, then, like He did with the woman, He would have raised them up in their humility to a higher level, one marked by His forgiveness and mercy. But they all went away instead.

Conclusion

Whether we lift ourselves up or lower ourselves below, Christ is there, right alongside us, inviting us to come to Him, offering us His yoke, making Himself weak so that we can be evenly yoked with Him, not in spite of our weakness, our infirmity, and our sin, but because of it. To accept His yoke is to accept and bring our weaknesses to Him so that He can heal us, forgive us, and make us His own. If we submit to Him in this way and share His yoke and His light and easy burden, then we will be filled with His love and we will carry that love alongside Him into the world. This is perfection in Christ: to love with His love, which is a whole, all-inclusive, and even love, and it is this love that He commands of us in Matthew 5:48.

CHAPTER 4

Toward a More Perfect Marital Union

You come to love not by finding the perfect person, but by learning to see an imperfect person perfectly.

—*Sam Keen*

Kathy's Story

One evening when I returned home from shopping, my husband, Larry, met me at the door, grinning. *What's he up to?* I wondered. He led me into the kitchen and announced, "I did the dishes for you!" As I hugged him and exclaimed, "Thank you!" I looked over his shoulder and noticed crumbs and drops of liquid on the counter. *But you haven't wiped the counter*, I thought. *You haven't finished the dishes!* Before I could chastise him, I remembered how my struggles with perfectionism and impatience robbed me of enjoying and appreciating my wonderful husband. I thanked him *again*, determined not to allow his "mistakes" to bother me. The next evening Larry did the dishes again. I realized he wouldn't have washed them a second time if I'd criticized him the day before. I witnessed again the power of affirming his attempts—even if they didn't meet my expectations.

Someone once said that a perfectionist is a person who takes great pains and passes them on to others. I would have given my husband a great pain that evening if I'd discounted his effort. Yet that's exactly what perfectionism does: It brings pain and destruction to our lives and marriages. Throughout the first seven years of our marriage, I struggled with perfectionist tendencies. Nothing Larry did was good enough. He wasn't a good enough provider—even though he worked two jobs to support our family while I stayed home with the kids. He didn't talk enough to me; he didn't help properly with the housework; he wasn't as concerned about my desires and expectations as I was. The list went on and on. My standards were set so high that Larry couldn't win—ever. Since Larry didn't meet all my needs, I believed I couldn't give him credit when he showed me love. Instead I focused on his inadequacies. No matter how Larry tried to please me, I found fault and pointed out his shortcomings to "motivate" him. I "punished" him with my displeasure by withholding sex, affection, joy"[1] (Miller, 2008).

This excerpt from Kathy's story poignantly demonstrates what happens in a marriage when the language of perfectionism is the only language spouses know. As you can see in the first paragraph, even though Kathy learned some coping strategies, her perfectionism remained front and center in her mind and

1 Kathy Collard Miller, author of *Why Do I Put So Much Pressure on Myself and Others?* www.kathycollardmiller.com.

heart. She still noticed the crumbs and drops of liquid on the counter, and she continued to evaluate those things as flaws in her husband that demonstrated his inadequacy in completing the task. She coped with this by determining within herself not to be bothered by these mistakes, and she made sure to catch herself before chastising him. However, at this point in her story, she remains a perfectionist, albeit a less outspoken one.

Fortunately, Kathy's story does not end there. After seven years of living perfectionistically, falling out of love with her husband because he failed to meet her high expectations, and then trying to cope with all of that by holding her tongue, Kathy was exposed to an alternative language of perfection, a properly Christian language of perfection. Kathy writes, "One day, during my devotions, God opened my eyes to what I was doing." Kathy, who, like all of us, was incapable of finding a way out of the vise grip of perfectionism by her own efforts, was shown the more perfect way. And what is the more perfect way that she was shown? Kathy answers that question through an experience. She reports that one day while cleaning the house:

> I sensed God say, "Tell Larry you love him." I was shocked. *No!* I thought. *I don't love Larry.* My unmet expectations had squelched my love—because love and a perfectionist attitude can't really coexist. *Besides,* I thought, *I haven't said those words to him in more than two years. If I say them now, he might think I approve of his negligence toward me and the kids.* In my perfectionistic thinking, since I didn't feel love for Larry all the time, I couldn't say I loved him. Finally, I felt God whisper, "Think it the next time you see Larry." *That's strange,* I thought. *But if he doesn't hear me, then he can't use it against me. All right, Lord, I'll do it, even if it isn't true.*

That evening when Larry returned, I stared at him, gulped, and thought, *I love you...but I don't really*. Even though I obeyed God begrudgingly, an amazing thing happened. Over the following months, as I continued to think the words *I love you* whenever I looked at Larry, I began to *feel* love for him. I also recognized that I'd been holding Larry responsible for my happiness. As I received grace for myself and then offered it to Larry, my "all or nothing" thinking changed. I accepted the truth that Larry couldn't meet all my needs—only God could. In time, Larry noticed that I wasn't as angry and demanding. And our marriage became more comfortable and enjoyable for both of us.

God exposed Kathy to the language of His perfect love. At first, she resisted this alternative and only practiced it begrudgingly. The language was so foreign, so unfamiliar. It just did not ring true. However, as she practiced speaking it, even if only in her mind, her heart changed. She allowed God's love in, and through the grace of His love, her love for her husband grew and their marriage improved. It was not easy. It did not happen overnight. Surely, she still falls back into her primary language of perfectionism all the time. But now she knows there is another way to be perfect, another language she can speak, and she knows it is the Lord's way because it came directly from Him.

The Paradox of Perfectionism in Marriage

We have seen many couples in counseling, like Kathy and her husband, who are schematic for perfectionism. They fixate on the flaws in their marriage and see them as the source of all their troubles. They think, "If our communication was not so poor, then we would have a better marriage. If he was not at work all the time, then we would have a better marriage. If the kids were not always creating stress, then our marriage would be better. If her parents would stop meddling in our marriage, then it would be better." They come to counseling hoping that we will help them remove one failure, one weakness, or one flaw in their marriage with each session, and they believe that once the imperfections of the marriage are removed, then they will be happy, satisfied, and finally pleased with their union.

The paradox of this perfectionistic view of marriage is that the more spouses pursue the removal of weaknesses and flaws from their marriages, the less available they make their marriages to the grace and redemptive power of the Savior. The more they pursue flawlessness, the further they remove themselves from what should be the proper focus of their marriage: filling their marriage with the love of God so that their marriage is whole, complete, and even. Too many husbands and wives focus on how they can get themselves or their partners to become an ideal mate, when they should be focused on coming to Christ and becoming yoked together with Him.

The Imperfect Marriage

Obviously, given the very different view of weaknesses and flaws we have discussed, we do not think a marriage is made imperfect by faults, failings, and errors. And we do not think it is perfected by flawlessness. Quite the opposite, in fact: We see marital mistakes, frailty, and sins as access points for Christ's grace and mercy. If that is the case, then what makes a marriage imperfect? A marriage is made imperfect when it is not filled with the love of God, and the love of God will not be present, as Kathy's story demonstrates, when the relationship between the participants in the marriage is not level and even.

To illustrate our point, consider the pie chart below. In 1 Corinthians 11:11, Paul teaches, "Neither is the man without the woman, neither the woman without the man, in the Lord." We believe this is true of all men and women in all relationships of which they are a part, but it is an essential truth of Christian marriage. So, a marriage "in the Lord" may be depicted as looking something like this:

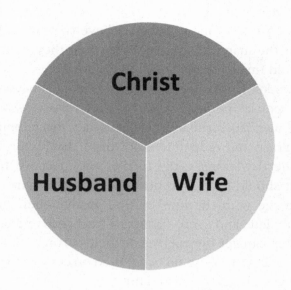

All three participants are necessary. All three participants have a place or a role in the marriage, and if any member of the marriage is missing, the marriage is not complete and whole. But there is more to this pie chart than meets the eye. In its current view, this pie chart suffers from one-dimensionality. Marriages, like all other relationships, have multiple dimensions, and one dimension that is very important to perfection is the vertical dimension, the dimension of height and depth. If we lay this pie chart on its back, we can see that the husband, the wife, and Christ are not just components of the whole, but that when a marriage is "in the Lord," they are also all on an even plane. That means that if this disk were an object you were holding, you could run your finger over its surface and you would feel no unevenness along the borders between the pie pieces. All of the parts would be smooth and level with each other.

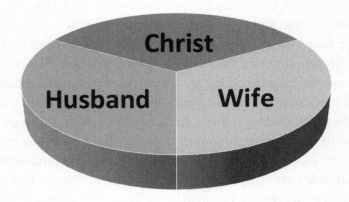

Imperfection would occur in this marital pie chart if one of these slices of the pie were to be raised above or lowered beneath the others. For example, if a husband believes he is superior to his wife due to any attribute, then he is acting as if his piece of the pie has become elevated over his wife's, and as a result he, his wife, and Christ will not be equally yoked.

Recall Kathy's feelings about her husband during the first seven years of their marriage. From her perspective at that time, he was never good enough, never adequate, always falling below her expectations. After reading her critique, it might appear that his piece of the pie was lower than her piece because of his faults and flaws, but, in fact, it is her pie piece that moved. She elevated herself above him (and Christ, as we will see) by pretending that she did not share in such failings. Clearly, she saw herself as the superior dish washer, but she also appointed herself as her husband's judge and critic. She even perceived herself to be his trainer, teaching him how to act by punishing his bad behavior and reinforcing his good behavior. She had to tolerate *his* mistakes and try not to be bothered by *his* errors. She makes no mention of her own faults. He alone was the disappointment, not her. Clearly, at that time in their marriage, she was placing herself above him, with her only acknowledged flaw being that she was perfectionistic and expected too much of him.

Kathy is not alone. We all do this on regular occasion. One spouse may lord his education over the other. Another may consider herself superior because she is the primary breadwinner. Still another may think his spouse lucky to even have him as a partner because he is more physically attractive and could be with so many other partners. In a church context, it is easy for a spouse to feel more righteous than her partner, who may struggle more obviously with obedience to certain commandments. In the horrible case of spousal abuse, a husband may assume superiority over his spouse because he is physically stronger than she is. The list goes on and on. There are likely an infinite number of ways we can lift ourselves above each other in our marriages.

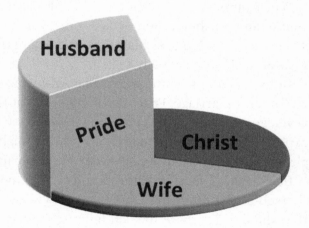

Lifted Up in Pride

At its core, all of the ways in which we feel superior to our spouse are born of pride and arrogance. When we are proud, we are "puffed up" (1 Corinthians 4:6) as Paul described it. We make ourselves feel and appear larger than we actually are, and we act as if we are greater than the people around us. But, alas, it is all only hot air. It is only pretense, but pretense is enough to make a marriage uneven and imperfect, meaning devoid of the love of God. Think about it, can you really love your spouse when you feel superior to him or her? Can you truly feel God's love in your heart when you are lifted up in self-righteousness and arrogance?

You cannot feel God's love in your proud position, because the source of God's love is Christ and Christ will not join you in that elevated posture, for He "is meek and lowly in heart" (Matthew 11:29 kjv). Without God's love inhabiting us, we are left to our own devices and we are ruled by our own emotions, which will always be contingent, partial, and incomplete. Recall how Kathy felt toward her husband when she was lifted up in her perfectionistic pride. She felt disappointment and she felt anger, but she could not feel love. And, though she told herself it was Larry's fault that she did not love him, it was not. It was the height she created between her and her Lord that led to love's departure from her heart and contributed to a marriage that was not even, filled with love, and perfect.

Sunken Down in Despair

On the other side of the spectrum, we find despair. Despair lowers us beneath our spouse and beneath Christ, as we judge ourselves unworthy of our loved one and of our God because of sin, frailty, and inadequacy. Imagine Larry's side of Kathy's story. It would be easy for him to feel despair as he continues to disappoint her by failing to live up to her expectations. Indeed, he did report in her story that "I used to think, *Kathy is never satisfied no matter what I do, so I might as well give up trying to please her.*" Feeling like there is no hope and giving up are common characteristics of despair. We can also experience despair and lower ourselves beneath our spouse when we compare ourselves to him or her, which often means comparing our weaknesses to his or her strengths. This can lead to jealousy and self-deprecation, as well as efforts to make our spouse feel guilty or ashamed for being "better" than we are.

When we despair over our inadequacies, our sins, and our failings, we make ourselves uneven with Christ. We try to convince ourselves that we do not deserve His love, that somehow we have found a dark corner of the universe where His mercy and grace cannot reach us. By so doing, we unyoke ourselves from Him and we are not filled with His love and light. Once we separate ourselves from Christ in that self-deprecating way, then, just like those puffed up in pride, we are left to our own petty and partial emotions. Our countenance darkens, regret and shame saturate our souls, and we become depressed and hopeless. Like the woman caught in adultery, we expect to be despised and we feel we deserve harsh punishment and no forgiveness. We look downward in shame and have no hope of redemption. In such a state, we can hardly make a genuine and meaningful contribution to our marriage, because we think we have nothing of value or worth to offer.

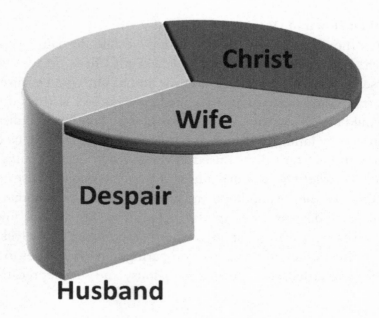

The Pride/Despair Dynamic

As awful as the distance created by pride and despair can be in their own right, the distance between husband and wife and the Lord can grow even greater when one spouse is lifted up in pride and the other is down in the depths of despair. In fact, marriages often suffer from a dynamic in which husband and wife simultaneously raise and lower themselves in relation to each other across a variety of domains.

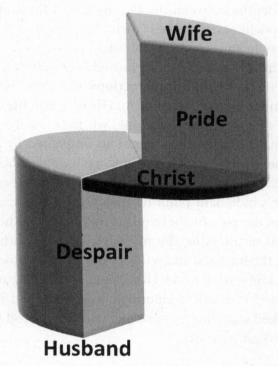

One example of this dynamic that we see often in our clients of faith is what we label the Pharisee and the sinner dynamic. As we have already noted, the Pharisees of Christ's time were renowned for their pride. They lifted themselves up above all others as they obeyed the Law most purely and most excellently. The sinners whom the Pharisees encountered did not just feel the depth of their sinfulness in relation to their God. The depth of their despair sunk even lower in comparison to the Pharisees, who appeared so much more elevated and more holy than they could ever be. This contrast was reinforced in the other direction, as well. That is, the more the Pharisees could see the filthiness of the sinners around them, the more pride they could feel in the purity they practiced.

Neither of these groups may have consciously initiated this dynamic, but once it was set in place, it surely facilitated greater heights and depths between the Pharisees and the sinners than would have taken place on their own. And, most sadly, neither the Pharisees nor the sinners in this vicious cycle were even and level with Christ. They had both moved themselves away from Him and His love in opposite directions and were living off of their own emotions rather than from His light and life.

In our couples' therapy sessions, we have rarely seen one spouse feeling inferior who was not accompanied by a partner who felt superior. On many occasions we have watched and listened as one spouse bows his or her head in shame beneath the other spouse's indignant pointing finger. As this dynamic plays out, it pushes the pair further and further apart, to the point of possibly even terminating the marriage. In their suffering and desperation, the husband and wife cry out one last time for help. They do not know what to do. How could they? They are relying wholly on their own fallen emotions, judgment, and ideas, and in that unyoked state they cannot feel the love of God for themselves or for their partners.

"My Ways Are Not Your Ways"

Because spouses who are caught up in these un-leveling dynamics rely on their own fallen thoughts and feelings, their imagined solutions to these relational problems are often either very egoistic or overly altruistic. We can easily see the egoistic approach in Kathy's story. When she was speaking only the language of perfectionism, she saw the problems in her marriage as being Larry's fault and she saw her own personal unhappiness as the effect of his flaws. If he would just live up to her expectations, then she would feel better, she would be happier, and she would love him more. Larry could just as easily assert that if Kathy would just come down off her high horse and admit that she, too, came up short, just as he did, then he could get some relief from her constant judgment and criticism.

Here, then, is the common egoistic refrain: If the husband would just change for the wife or if the wife would just change for the husband, then the issues between them would go away and all would be well. And, after all, isn't it right and proper to expect that if my spouse really loved me, then he or she would want to change for me? This idea may seem reasonable to us. It is a common theme and expectation in our culture of romanticized love. But this is the egoistic reasoning of a fallen people who can easily forget that God's thoughts and God's ways are different than our own (Isaiah 55:8). Indeed, such egoistic reasoning is clearly altogether different from God's, because it leaves Christ out of the equation and as a result cannot make husband and wife even "in the Lord."

On the other side of the coin, we have seen many spouses adopt what appears to be an altruistic approach to their uneven marriages. In one meeting in which we were teaching about being level in our marriages, a woman raised her hand and reported that her husband had a pornography problem and then sincerely asked if she should start looking at pornography, too, even though she didn't want to, so that she and her spouse would be more even. Similarly, we have worked with people who drink in overabundance so they can be more like their alcoholic husband or wife and help them not feel so badly about their addiction and being alone in it.

These efforts to sacrifice one's own morals and mental and physical health for the sake of a spouse are intended to make spouses even, albeit in sin and vice, but they do not make spouses even with the Lord. Like egoistic approaches, they do not focus on and include the Savior. The leveling is treated as a matter of what "I" can do to be level with my spouse rather than what Christ can do to make us level with Him. This is a consequence of the thinking of a fallen mind that is bound up with and hindered by the schema and language of perfectionism. But what else can be done when the language of perfectionism is the only language that we speak?

The Perfect Marriage

The answer to this question, as we have described it already, is that we have to learn a new language of perfection and then let that language guide and inspire our marriages as often as possible. We have to learn God's thoughts and His ways; we have to learn the language of His perfect love. The key to learning this language and filling our marriages with God's love is not found in our fallen ideas and absurd egoistic or altruistic attempts to make ourselves even with our spouse. Joining our spouse in pride or in despair may make us appear more even as a pair, but it will not make us level with Christ, and it will not last. Our marriages will be incomplete. They will not be "in the Lord," because the Lord is neither proud nor despairing. He is humble and hopeful. As a God from on high who descended below all things, He surely understands our pride and despair, and He will reach out to us in those higher or lower positions we pretend to occupy, but He will not join us there. Instead, He invites us to come unto Him, where He resides in meekness and lowliness of heart. Only then, if both husband and wife accept Christ's invitation and come to Him on His level, can their marriage be made complete and even, perfect.

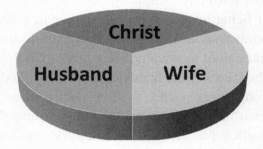

Christ entices husband and wife to come unto Him and be made perfect or level with Him in many ways. Recall that Kathy felt God's invitation in the form of a command to express love to her husband. You may experience God's invitation to come unto Him when you read the Bible, attend church, or sing a hymn. In our own marriages and in our work as therapists, we have seen the Lord's invitation to couples to come unto Him manifest in a typical and often powerful way that we want to review in detail here.

Equal in Sin

First, the Lord invites husband and wife to acknowledge that they both are sinners. They may not indulge the same sins, engage in their respective sinful behaviors at the same pace, or consider their respective sins equivalent in severity. But that does not ultimately matter before God, for regardless of the specifics, *"all* we like sheep have gone astray" (Isaiah 53:6) and *"all* have sinned and come short of the glory of God" (Romans 3:23). In this sense, sin is the great equalizer, or leveler. It places all people in the same position before God. As a result, husbands and wives cannot honestly lift themselves above their spouses in any form of self-righteousness, for God cannot tolerate sin in even the least degree, meaning that no sinner of any type is worthy or deserving of God's salvation by his or her own merits. By the same token, neither spouse has more claim upon despair than the other, for both have stumbled and lost their way. Thus, any pretense of being uneven with each other in regard to worthiness, righteousness, and sin is born of a failure to acknowledge that sin makes all of us equally fallen before God.

Remember the woman from our class who asked if she should start watching pornography with her husband so she could be more level with him? The problems with her question are many, but one significant issue is that her inquiry implied that she was not already level with him and that participating in the watching of pornography would initiate the leveling. It is true that he might have a pornography problem and she might not, but she had other issues, other sins, that might differ in type from his. Her sins make no difference in the position they place her in relation to God and salvation, which is right alongside her husband and all of us together falling short of His glory.

Though sin places husbands and wives, along with everyone else, on equal footing as fallen sinners before our God, it does not perfect our marriages. Our marriages are not yet "in the Lord" because in our sins we have not yet come unto Him and taken His yoke upon us. Still, acknowledging our sins and the equal position in which they place all of us before God, regardless of their type, frequency, or severity, is a necessary first step in the leveling and perfecting of our marriages. At the very least, it destroys the pretense of the pride/despair dynamic exemplified by the Pharisees and the sinners that presses husbands and wives in opposite directions and exacerbates the distance between them and the Lord. This pretense is itself a sin; it is a relational sin shared by the husbands and wives who participate in it, and it, too, must be redeemed, together with the individual sins for which husbands and wives are accountable, if they are to be married "in the Lord" and perfected in Him.

Relational Repentance

The need for individual and relational redemption brings in the second feature of Christ's invitation to come unto Him, which is His invitation to repent. Repentance is the primary means by which we come unto Christ and are yoked to Him. Christ, who did not sin, but who took upon Himself all of our sins so that He could succor us, comes down to our fallen and corrupted level and meets us there, just as He met the woman caught in adultery, kneeling beside her on the ground. But He does not stay and wallow in sin with us. He extends His hand to us, and if we take hold of His hand of mercy and grace, then He lifts us up out of the muck and the mire into the bright light of His love. As husband and wife turn to Christ, confess their sins, and accept His mercy, they are made level not only with Christ, but also with each other. But the sins they must confess and give over to Christ are not only the individual sins they each commit, but also the relational sins that sully their marriage. Thus, it is only when both individual and relational repentance is practiced that a truly even and perfect marriage "in the Lord" can be achieved.

One of the most powerful experiences we have witnessed in our work with couples of faith is being present as a husband and wife cry out to God together in prayer, asking Him to heal their broken and sinful relationship, begging Him to replace a dynamic of anger and hostility with one of joy and kindness. They are praying not only for the husband or only for the wife, but for their relationship, for "us." As they offer up their relationship on the altar of repentance, God's Spirit is present and palpable, hearts begin to soften, and love begins to replace hate and indifference. No one stands above or below the other. At that moment, husband, wife, and God are all even and level in a relationship marked by humility, meekness, and kindness. The marriage is filled with God's love and made whole and complete. Indeed, it is at that time, perfect.

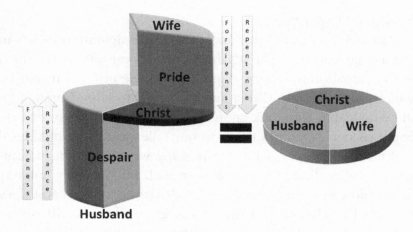

A Foundation of Forgiveness

Relational repentance is crucial to an even and whole marriage in the Lord. Yet there remains one final and crucial step in the leveling process. The final feature of this common invitation to couples to come unto Christ and be made even with Him is found in the Lord's invitation to forgive. It is perhaps a sad truth, depending on your perspective, that the person who can hurt us most in the world, and who often does so, is our husband or wife. Many of us would like to think that our chosen life partner would never injure us in any way, or would at least do so less than other people with whom we are less intimately connected. However, we know, from personal experience and from research data and even crime statistics, that spouses do hurt each other more than others, and they do so across physical, emotional, psychological, and spiritual dimensions. Some of these injuries are unintentional and may result from insensitivity or a lack of empathy, while others are intentionally designed to hurt the partner. In short, couples sin against each other all the time, and they often do so with each other more than they sin in any other relationship.

Perfectionistic partners have little tolerance for these marital sins. They think that spouses who truly love each other would never cause each other suffering, especially not intentionally. If spouses do hurt their partners, then they must not have truly loved their partners and therefore they do not deserve the marriage. We saw in Kathy's story that in her perfectionism, she discounted Larry's love for her. She thought that if Larry really loved her, then he would change for her and become a more perfect husband. When the changes did not come, at least not to her satisfaction, then she took that as an indication that he must not really love her, and she felt justified in falling out of love with him. This perfectionistic attitude and the fantasy of flawlessness that fuels it makes forgiveness nearly impossible. It promotes the false belief that there should be no need for forgiveness to begin with because no wrongdoing should ever take place in a marriage marked by true love. It also facilitates the fallacious idea that if wrongdoing does take place, then the spouse's love and the love inhabiting the marriage is not genuine.

Unfortunately, these beliefs are publicly reinforced all the time. On several occasions, we have heard people proudly state from the pulpit at their church or in a Sunday school class that they have never raised their voice at their spouse or had a fight in their marriage. Their intention, it would appear, is to model a most excellent marriage, one based in "true love" and one approximating the goal of flawlessness for which they believe we ought to all strive. But the effect of their perfectionistic comment, as we will discuss in greater detail in chapter 6, is that they make themselves uneven with their fellow parishioners, many of whom do yell at their partners and have had fights, even big fights, on numerous occasions. Instead of encouraging the audience with their most excellent model of perfection, their comment causes heads to bow in shame and spouses to question whether they married the "right" person.

Comments like these do not bring the audience closer to Christ, and they do not strengthen their faith. On the contrary, they can weaken a couple's relationship to Christ and to each other as they compare and question the truthfulness of their love and the worthiness of their marriage. It teaches spouses that for-giveness is for couples who lack genuine love. It is for the lesser marriages, weaker marriages. What a shame this is! Instead of seeing the practice of marital forgiveness as a wonderful blessing from God and an opportunity for couples to become whole and even with Him, they view it as an unwanted consolation prize for marital failure, like the green ribbon kids dread receiving simply because they participated in an event.

Obviously, given our discussion of weakness in chapter 3, we have a very different perspective. We do not see marital weak-nesses as indicators that our love is untrue at all. Rather, mari-tal weaknesses are the key access points for the Savior's grace, mercy, and love to enter into our marriages. We are not saying that marital sins, like yelling and fighting, are wonderful things and we ought to seek them out. We are strongly asserting that weaknesses like these, which are a part of any marriage, signify, among many other indicators, that marriages, like individuals, are fallen and depend wholly on the Savior for their redemption and well-being. Marital frailties and infirmities give the Healer something to heal and provide forgiving spouses the opportunity to be filled with God's love, which is precisely what makes our marital love true and genuine.

We can both say without hesitation that many of the most sig-nificant moments of our marriages, the times when the love we shared with our spouses has been the strongest and the truest, have centered on forgiveness. And the moments of forgiveness that have had the greatest marital impact have often been those in which the forgiveness was not deserved or even asked for. It was given freely as a gift of love from the Savior, and it filled the heart of the forgiver and was then extended without resistance. What a precious opportunity forgiveness can be! It can recon-cile spouses to each other and to God, binding us together in His love, which is the only true and genuine love we can know.

Why would we resist the opportunity to experience Christ's love? We should not despise the opportunity because it is born of suffering or injury and requires forgiveness of one or both of us. His love is the greatest gift we can receive, and we can and should do whatever is needed to have it in our marriages, including forgiving our spouses, even when they are undeserving of it. Forgiveness fills us with light and lightens our burden, freeing us of bitterness and of guilt, and leveling us with one another as we acknowledge that none of us stands above or below the other. Because we all depend wholly on His mercy and grace, we must be forthcoming with our forgiveness because we have no right to withhold it or to judge our spouse unworthy of it. It is His to give, and we make ourselves uneven with Him and with each other when our stubbornness hinders the extension of His love to our spouse.

Conclusion

Marriages are not made imperfect by our flaws. They are made imperfect by our resistance to the love of God. That resistance takes hold when a spouse's flaws are flaunted and used as justification for self-righteous pride, when one's own flaws are seen to connote unworthiness and facilitate self-deprecating despair, or when marital flaws are taken as evidence that spouses' love for each other must not be true or genuine. Marriages are perfected when marital flaws and weaknesses are valued as essential access points for the love of God, when they equalize us in sin, and when they help us accept the always extended hand of the Lord through repentance and forgiveness. In a perfect marriage, husband, wife, and God are evenly yoked under the divine love of the great Healer, whose balm alone can salve marital wounds. And it is in those moments of repentance and forgiveness, when as couples we are level "in the Lord," that we are obeying Christ's command to be perfect, even as our Father who is in heaven is perfect.

CHAPTER 5

Parental Perfection

To consign children to the pursuit of perfection is to trap them in an illusion.

—*Hara Estroff Marano*

The language of perfectionism is perhaps no more pervasively spoken than it is in our homes with our children. Maybe it is because our children share our genes, so we identify their successes and failures with our own. Perhaps it is because parents play such a formative role in their children's development that we feel personally culpable for their thoughts, feelings, and actions. Whatever the reason, many parents' self-esteem is tied up with the achievements, shortcomings, and reputations of their children, and they will work tirelessly to identify and remove their children's flaws and faults so they can feel better about themselves (Reber & Moody, 2013). Given this tendency, we would suggest that if perfectionism is not the very first language many children hear and learn in their homes, it is pretty darn close.

The Pursuit of Perfect Children

Even before a child is born, many parents hope for a baby without blemish, a baby who is even-tempered, and a baby who is cute and cuddly. And some parents, if they are being honest, evaluate those things from the moment they see their baby for the first time. Of course, nowadays it is possible to increase the probability of having an unblemished, cute, and cuddly baby. A woman can choose a mate or a sperm donor according to his IQ scores, athletic prowess, physical attractiveness, musical and artistic talent, or educational degree and career success.

Beyond that, science and technology have taken what used to be the stuff of science fiction and turned it into a bona-fide business. Now parents can select their offspring's biological sex as well as their eye color, and perhaps within as little as five to ten years, they will likely be able to choose their child's approximate adult height and weight. For the last thirty years, the Chinese government has supported the largest eugenics program in the world. Currently, China is working on a massive project designed to identify the gene alleles correlated with high intelligence, for the purpose of allowing parents to select potential offspring who are most likely to have the highest IQs.

We can't help but be reminded of the now clearly prescient 1992 movie *Gattaca*, which depicts a not-so-futuristic society in which genetic engineering has become the norm. We are particularly struck by the relevance of the scene where two parents sit with their local geneticist and view two male and two female embryos made from the father's sperm and the mother's eggs on a computer screen, from which they will choose the one they want. The geneticist tells them that he has taken "the liberty of eradicating any prejudicial conditions: premature baldness, myopia, alcoholism and addictive susceptibilities, propensity for violence, obesity..." The wife and husband look at each other with concern and interrupt the doctor, stating, "We didn't want. . . I mean, diseases yes, but...we were wondering if it's good to just leave a few things to chance." In a condescending and unbending tone, the doctor replies, "You want to give your child the best possible start. Believe me, we have enough imperfection built in already. Your child doesn't need any additional burdens. Keep in mind, this child is still you, simply the best of you. You could conceive naturally a thousand times and never get such a result."

Flawlessness versus Frailty

The doctor's rhetoric is cogent and the temptation is real. What if we could remove the physical, emotional, and psychological weaknesses that can disable, inhibit, and limit children? What if we could improve their strength, their intellect, and their attractiveness? If we could remove the limitations of nature, then we would only have to focus on nurture, which is hard enough in itself. Can you feel the perfectionism in you resonate with the possibilities, even if it feels kind of wrong, kind of like cheating? It makes sense, doesn't it? If you despise weakness and you see flaws as an unwanted burden, then you will do whatever you can to prevent them or to subdue them when they emerge. If you are schematic for perfectionism, then at the end of the day, eugenics in some form or another, and the natural excellence it promises, is kind of a no-brainer.

What if, on the other hand, you do not see faults and frailty as hindrances to the ideal form of a perfect child? What if you see flaws as opportunities for connection to Christ, as access points through which His love and mercy can inhabit your child's heart, mind, and soul, right along with yours? If you see your children in this way, then you will see the pursuit of flawlessness through programs of eugenics and other behavioral/genetic engineering endeavors as being potentially aversive to our relationship with the Savior. This is not to say that disabilities are wonderful things, any more than sins are desirable in and of themselves. They are, however, one of the vicissitudes of human life, and like the thorn in Paul's side, these infirmities can provide an opportunity for greater dependence on the One who seeks to succor us in our weakness and frailty, an opportunity not only for the child, but also an opportunity for the child's parents and siblings.

These two very different languages of perfection—one that despises frailty and one that embraces it—lead to very different implications and views of the world. Consider the experience of a pastor's wife and mother of a young boy diagnosed with autism. She reports that at a recent church potluck, a woman asked if her son was going to grow out of his autism, and then followed up with the question, "What did you do when you were pregnant to make him that way?" At another church activity, a different woman who observed her son asked, "Did you eat a lot of tuna when you were pregnant? I hear that's what causes those problems" (Peoples, 2014).

The language of perfectionism was clearly spoken by these two women, and the fact that they were somehow comfortable asking these insensitive and hurtful questions of the mother suggests that this may be the only language they know. Moreover, they clearly define the boy's autism as a problem and something to be outgrown. It is a flaw, a fault, and is therefore bad and unwanted. Not only that, they believe it must be a consequence of the mother's failure to have acted properly during her pregnancy. She must have done something wrong to create the disability. To their thinking, it is actually her fault, not the boy's. Unfortunately, all too commonly the mother would agree, for she too often only speaks the language of perfectionism, as was the case with another mother who lost two children soon after being born. She writes, "Like many people who experience difficulty, I immediately made the assumption that my suffering was my fault, that all my sins had caught up with me and I was finally getting what I deserved" (Peoples, 2014).

We, the authors, feel it necessary to state here that our concern with liberating people from the language of perfectionism and from the schema of flawlessness is greatest when it comes to parents, especially mothers. It breaks our hearts that people can speak so insensitively and hurtfully to a struggling mother as these two women did to the pastor's wife, but it breaks our hearts even more to know that some mothers feel the same concerns about themselves that these women expressed. The blame and self-recrimination are devastating to mothers already exhausted by the challenges of raising children, especially children with special needs. It is literally adding insult to injury, and it is not okay. It is not the Lord's way.

Fortunately, some mothers have found another way: "the way, the truth, and the life" (John 14:6), who is Christ, and they have learned another language of perfection as a result. One mother of a child diagnosed with Down syndrome speaks the language of perfection this way: "Penny is neither a rebuke nor a reward. She is a child, not a product of sin or of biological happenstance or of any lesson we needed to learn. No. This happened that the glory of God might be revealed" (Peoples, 2014). Speaking the language of perfect love, this parent understands that Penny, like every child, however that child comes to us, is an opportunity for the love of God to be felt and for the glory of God to be made manifest to the family and beyond. She knows that when families are bathed in that love of God, the family is made whole and even, complete and perfect in Christ.

Imperfect Parents

Because we, the authors, speak perfectionism so fluently, we already know how your perfectionistic mind works. We know that when you see the title of this section, "Imperfect Parents," you reflexively think of the mistakes parents make in general and the failures marking your own efforts to raise your children. That is okay; let those initial thoughts and feelings come in and then remember that flaws and faults do not make parents imperfect. No, imperfect parents, like imperfect spouses, are imperfect because they have become uneven with their children, and as a result they are also uneven with Christ and cannot be filled with His love and in turn love their children as He does.

You might think, "Wait a minute. Parents are inherently uneven with their children. We have to be. We are older and wiser than they are, and it is our responsibility to instruct them and discipline them, and if we do not do our job, we are bad parents." It is true; you are older than your children. You have had more experiences than they have had, and you may even be wiser than they are. It is also true that you have a legal and ethical obligation to care for your children, who are less capable of independence than you are. That is all accurate, but those differences are not what make us uneven with our children and our God. Being different from our children and having distinct roles and responsibilities in relation to our children is inevitable and desirable. Remember that Christ, too, is very different from us, and He has very different roles and responsibilities than we do, yet He allows Himself to be even with all of us.

What makes us uneven with our children is not our different roles and responsibilities as their parents, but the manner in which we take up those roles and responsibilities. Recall the pie chart from chapter 4, which we have modified to represent our parenting. Note that parents, children, and Christ are in perfect relationship when the pie pieces are level and all three parts are present in the whole. Put more scripturally, a family is perfect when parents and children have taken Christ's yoke upon them and now carry the light and easy burden of His love together. The family becomes imperfect when parents or children reject the yoke of the Savior by their pride and/or their despair. As parents, if we puff ourselves up to appear greater than our children or we think ourselves undeserving and unworthy of our children, then we move ourselves above them or below them, and as a result we leave our children behind and are not yoked with them and the Lord.

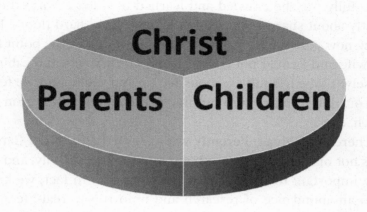

The Unleveling "Cs"

Care

Parents can reject the yoke of Christ and become uneven with their children and their God in many ways, but a familiar process or method stands out. This unleveling method begins with the first C, which is *Care*. Most parents care about their children. Even before they have children—in some cases, even before they are married—parents-to-be look forward to having children. They already care about how those children will do in life, how they will think and feel, and what they will experience. Even very young kids will imagine how many children they will have when they grow up, what their names will be, what they will do for a living, where they will live when they grow up, and so on. It seems we are almost hard-wired to care about our children.

When the day finally comes that our first child enters our lives, parental care becomes very real. We find ourselves immediately and inescapably concerned for their safety, their health, and their well-being. I recall feeling almost compelled to check on our firstborn several times a night when we brought her home, making sure she was breathing, comfortable, and sleeping peacefully. As she crawled and learned to walk, I worried constantly about sharp-cornered coffee tables and hard floors. Like many new parents, we baby-proofed our house to the point that my wife and I could not even get into our drawers and cabinets ourselves! We felt fully responsible for our child, and we felt it was our job to make sure nothing bad happened to her on our watch, ever.

There is nothing inherently wrong with the first C of Care. It does not make us uneven with our children necessarily, and it is very important to their healthy development. In fact, we know from an abundance of research and unfortunate real-life anecdotes, that children who do not receive care from parents and are neglected or abused instead often experience a whole host of potentially devastating psychological consequences and impairments. Children need care as much as they need nourishment, almost more. The risk with care, however, as we saw in the case of the new mother with OCD in chapter 2, is that care can push our sense of responsibility for our children into hyper-drive and facilitate fear.

Think about it: You do not fear what might happen to things about which you have no care. If our family's new puppy chews up a pair of old shoes that I do not wear anymore, then more power to her. I do not care about those shoes, and as a result I do not feel responsible for protecting the shoes from her. But if that puppy gets ahold of my nice new dress shoes, then, oh boy, that makes me angry. I am angry at her for chewing them, but I am angrier with myself for not keeping them safely away from her. I did not fulfill my responsibility to protect my shoes. So, what gets me out of bed checking on my puppy's whereabouts at night is not a concern for my old shoes, but my fear that I might have left my new dress shoes in the family room and the dog may have already sunk her sharp puppy teeth into their supple leather uppers.

So it goes with our children, but at a much higher degree of magnitude. Because we care so much for them, we feel responsible for protecting them and keeping them safe. In that state of heightened responsibility, our mind becomes more aware of and concerned about the myriad threats of injury, sickness, disability, and death facing our children. As our awareness increases, our fear grows stronger. To help us overcome our increasing fear, we ratchet up our caretaking and protective efforts, which makes us even more aware of potential threats to our children, including those not before considered. Our fears grow accordingly, and the cycle repeats itself again and again with the fear magnified more intensely each time. This is what happened to the new mother suffering from OCD. She was caught in a vicious spiral of ever-increasing caretaking to try to manage her ever-expanding fear for her baby's health and safety.

Certainty

As our fear intensifies, a second C, which is *Certainty*, can easily come into play. If we could just know for sure that everything with our children will be okay, then we would need not fear. If I could somehow know for sure that my daughter would not stop breathing in the middle of the night, I would not be afraid for her safety as she slept, and I would not feel like I had to go in and check on her, sometimes inadvertently waking her up, several times a night. Think again of eugenics and of the doctors and parents who seek to make sure that their children are free of genetic defects. If they could know of their genetic safety with certainty, then they would have no fear about a disability, disease, or disorder presenting itself at birth or later in their lives. Similarly, if I could be certain that my teenager would not have a car accident, injuring himself or someone else, then I would not have to worry every time he takes the car for a drive. Certainty, it would appear, would stop our fear cold.

If we cannot achieve exact certainty, can we at least approximate it? Can we get high probability or very good predictability? High probability might not stop our fear altogether, but it would certainly diminish it. Think of your own everyday experience. You live with the very high probability that the sun will rise tomorrow, that a giant asteroid is not going to crash into you when you step out of your house, and that a swarm of killer bees will not attack you as you go for a walk. There are so many areas of your life about which you have little or no fear, because you have high confidence in the predictability of highly probable and highly improbable events. You could be wrong about these things, but that is highly unlikely, so you go about your day with little worry about these remote possibilities.

Of course, children are not as predictable as the sunrise. Their behavior, even at a very young age, can be uncertain and even improbable. How many of us have gotten that dreaded phone call from a teacher or vice principal reporting that one of our children has done something in class that was completely out of character, or even within their character, but still unexpected? Alas, when it comes to children, certainty would seem to be a pipe dream, and even high probability and predictability can be hard to come by. So, fear remains and easily grows, while the fantasy of certainty tantalizes parents in the back of their minds.

Control

Many parents try to compensate for the natural uncertainty and unpredictability that goes along with raising children by applying a third C, which is *Control*. Control is any endeavor in which we engage that is designed to heighten probability and closer approximate certainty in order to decrease our fear. The more control we have over our children, the more certain we can be that they will be safe, and our fear can subside more easily. Many parents, like the young mother with OCD, try to control the environment in which their children find themselves. They baby-proof the home, they move to neighborhoods and schools known for their safety, they try to influence their kids' friendships, and they put software programs on their routers and computers that keep malicious and unsavory content outside of the home. By controlling their kids' surroundings, parents hope to reduce threats to their safety and well-being, achieve a modicum of certainty about the protection of their children, at least in the home, and reduce the fear that comes with caring for the children. Much of this is very reasonable protective behavior and these can be good practices for parents to follow.

Compulsion

However, for some parents controlling the environment provides insufficient certainty to allay their fears, so they ratchet up their control by also trying to coerce or compel their children's behavior. Thus, *Compulsion* becomes the fourth and final C in this unleveling process. Compulsion is a common feature of a parenting style that developmental psychologists describe as authoritarian. When parents practice this style, they demand complete obedience from their children, and if they do not receive it, then their punishment is swift and severe. Sociologist Michael Dyson (2014) sheds light on authoritarian parenting by drawing a distinction between discipline, which is instructive but not coercive, and punishment, which is designed to hurt and compel. "The point of discipline," he states, "is to transmit values to children. The purpose of punishment is to coerce compliance and secure control, and failing that, to inflict pain as a form of revenge, a realm the Bible says belongs to God alone."

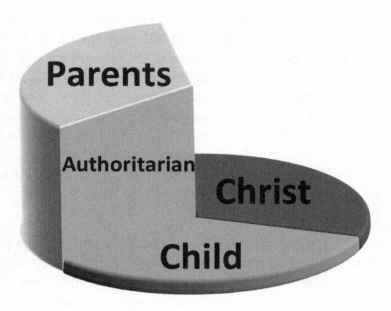

Usurping God's Authority

One can see easily in Dyson's description how an authoritarian approach to parenting can easily make parents uneven with their children, as they lift themselves above the children as dictators who will punish and exact revenge upon the children for their disobedience. When we parent in this manner, we also make ourselves uneven with Christ. Indeed, we may not realize it, but when we engage in coercive behavior we attempt to depose God, making us, the parents (not the children, and not God), ultimately responsible for the children's actions and life outcomes. This pretense of claiming God's authority for oneself is what C.S. Lewis describes as the original sin devised by Satan:

> What Satan put into the heads of our remote ancestors was the idea that they "could be like Gods"—could set up on their own as if they had created themselves—be their own masters—invent some sort of happiness for themselves outside God, apart from God. And out of that hopeless attempt has come...the long terrible story

of man trying to find something other than God which
will make him happy. (Lewis, 1952)

The attempt to usurp God's ultimate responsibility for another person's life, even a young and seemingly helpless child's life, is a form of pride based in fear and lacking in faith in God who is the Father of all spirits and the Keeper of our souls. In John 10, Jesus reminds us repeatedly that He alone is our Shepherd and we are His sheep, and He warns thieves, robbers, and even hirelings (e.g., parents) that no one can replace Him in that role. In verses 27 through 29, for example, He makes His irreplaceable responsibility for all of us very clear: "My sheep hear my voice, and I know them, and they follow me: And I give unto them eternal life; and they shall never perish, neither shall any man pluck them out of my hand. My Father, which gave them me, is greater than all; and no man is able to pluck them out of my Father's hand." Our children are ultimately in God's hand, not in ours. We guide and teach and discipline our children, and we point our children to the Good Shepherd and teach them to hear His voice, but we are not responsible for saving them, not even from themselves.

Abdicating Parental Responsibility
On the seemingly opposite side of the compulsion spectrum is a style of parenting described by developmental psychologists as permissive. When we practice permissive parenting, we do not take the time or put in the effort to discipline and teach our children. We might do this because we believe the children know better than we do what is best for them. We might be permissive as a form of indulging or spoiling our children. Or, in more extreme cases of neglect, we may just leave them basically on their own, because, we tell ourselves, they need to figure life out by themselves. Sometimes we just feel too lazy or too selfish to give parenting the attention it demands, and we leave the children to their own devices.

On the face of it, permissive parenting and perfectionism do not seem connected, but in our experience, we have found that parents who tend to practice a permissive approach to parenting are often no less perfectionistic than those who typically practice an authoritarian approach. These parents are schematic for flawlessness just as much as their authoritarian counterparts, but they can see the writing on the wall. They know it is impossible to control everything that threatens a child's health, well-being, and safety, and they are painfully aware of their own parental weaknesses and inadequacies, which are many. They also recognize that a child cannot be compelled to faultlessness. So, instead of ratcheting up their efforts to gain more control by trying to coerce their children in everything they do, the parents relinquish any notion of responsibility altogether. They abdicate their parental stewardship because they know there is no way to get an outcome of flawlessness for their children.

Beneath their seemingly carefree permissiveness, then, often lies a deep discouragement and a belief that there is no chance of succeeding as a parent. Indeed, even prior to becoming a parent, many people expect that they will fail to raise their child right and well (meaning without making mistakes or causing the child to suffer). As we discussed in chapter 2, the guilt and pain of causing another person to suffer because of our faults is almost too much to bear. This is especially true when the person we have caused to suffer is an innocent child. So, too many parents-to-be give up on the whole prospect of parenting. Some run away. Others give the child to other parents who seem more likely to succeed in that role. A number do stick around and keep the child, but they are not really present as parents, not as guides and instructors who discipline and teach the child.

In the end, when we parent permissively, or in more extreme cases when we essentially abandon the prospect of parenting altogether, we pretend to lower ourselves beneath our children. We feel unqualified to raise our children and overwhelmed by the responsibilities associated with raising them. We think we do not deserve our children because we are not good enough for them. Above all else, we cannot stand the thought of hurting them and ruining their lives, so we cower before our children, too scared to try to parent them lest we get it wrong and do them irreparable harm.

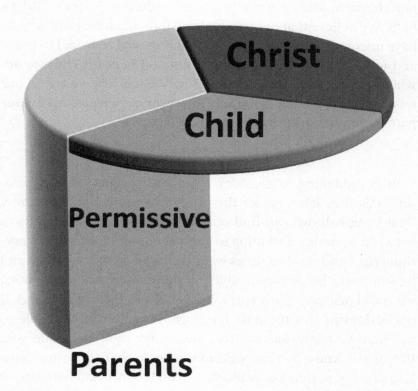

In this way (and just as was the case with authoritarian parenting), in our moments of permissive parenting, we overestimate our accountability for our children. We overattribute to ourselves the blame for their behaviors and for the course of their lives. We fail to remember that our children are first and foremost God's children, that they are ultimately in His hand,

and that He has the capacity to heal all of their wounds, including the wounds that parents inevitably inflict upon them.

Permissive parents' overattribution of responsibility is not due to the pride accompanying authoritarianism and it is not a conscious attempt to usurp Christ's responsibility. Instead, in our permissiveness, we overestimate our blameworthiness for our children, often because we feel we do not deserve Christ's help. We believe that our parental and individual sins and defects have uncoupled us from His yoke and removed us from His grace and mercy, and now, apart from Him and beneath Him we are wholly accountable for our parenting. We feel like we are on our own, and that feeling is too much to bear, so we give up on our parental duties and we let our children go.

Perfect Parents

It is saddening to consider how hard parents are on themselves as they labor under the burden of perfectionism. Like a Ping-Pong ball, we can find ourselves bouncing back and forth between sometimes wanting to compel our children to do everything right and at other times wanting to run away from them and let someone else be responsible for them for a while. As authors, we could just say, "Hey, sorry, but those are the breaks!" and, if perfectionism was the only language of perfection available to us, then we might just say that and suffer right alongside you. But, as you know by this point in the book, there are alternative languages of perfection available to us. The Christian language of charity, which Christ commands of us, provides an alternative to this misery, a different approach to parenting that does, indeed, allow for perfection.

The key to perfect parenting, from this uniquely Christian perspective, is clearly described in 1 John 4:18, which reads, "There is no fear in love; but perfect love casteth out fear: because fear hath torment. He that feareth is not made perfect in love." Simply put, perfect parents have perfect love and fearful parents do not. Perfect parents, despite all their inadequacies, their pride, and their despair, have accepted Christ's invitation to partnership, and they have yoked themselves to Him. As a result, they are filled with His pure love. This divine love that Christ alone can bring into our frail human hearts then emanates out from the parents into their interactions with each of their children, and it purges the parents' hearts and minds of fear.

Mindful of Fear and Its Torment

Make no mistake about it, it is our fear, as John taught, that torments us as we see all that can go wrong with our children. It is fear that leads us to either desire or abandon the ideal of control over our children. Parents may tell themselves and their children that they are parenting them with an authoritarian or permissive style because they love them and because it is for their own good. But when beneath it all there is not God's perfect love, but fear, then it is that fear that frightened and worried parents will inevitably pass along to their children, even if they do not intend to do so. Their children will then learn to live by fear. They will fear any grade lower than an A, they will be appalled by any sin that might tarnish their record of righteousness, and they will hate any physical, psychological, or spiritual disabilities they may have. In our fear, we teach our children fear-based perfectionistic language, and too often, we teach them only this language, making it difficult for them to see any other way to live, including the Living Way who is Christ.

Fear also breeds unevenness in our children. It can lead children who are subjected to the exacting strictness of authoritarian parenting to lower themselves beneath their parents, feeling like they can never live up to their parents' impossible expectations. Too often, these children consign themselves to the belief that they will always be hopeless failures and disappointments. Children of permissive parents may also become uneven with their parents. Too often, they become entitled and lifted up in narcissism and hubris, thinking they know better than their parents, other people, and even God.

We can guess what you are doing right now. You are reading these things and finding fault in your parenting. You are worrying that you have passed fear-based perfectionism on to your children and that it may be too late to change it. Some of you are thinking that maybe you have been too hard on your kids, too strict and demanding, and now they will forever feel inadequate. Others of you wonder if you may have raised little narcissists who will live life thinking the world is their oyster.

Now, before you head down the shame spiral, stop for a moment and take a few deep breaths. Notice the fear that is welling up in you, the anxiety that is coming over your body and the worry occupying your mind. Acknowledge it. Recognize the way it makes you feel in relation to your Lord and Savior. Observe how it makes you feel further away from Him, less deserving of His love, and unworthily beneath Him. Feel how your sense of responsibility is heightened and increasingly focused singularly on you, and note the temptation you feel toward controlling your children or running away from your parental responsibility. Hold all of that for just a moment.

Perfect Parental Love

Now close your eyes and let the image of Christ into your mind. See His face, note the look in His eyes, the line of His lips. Focus on Him, not on your children and not on yourself—just on Him. Hold the image. If you lose sight of it, that is okay; simply bring it back into your mind and focus on His face looking at you again. Take some time to do this before reading on. We are not going anywhere. We will be here when you are ready.

Now, after you have focused on the face of your Lord, allow yourself to think about how He treats, or we might say, how He parents you, not as a comparison to your own parenting, but as an exercise in appreciation and gratitude. Note that His parenting is always, without exception, marked by perfect love, meaning a love that is whole and complete in its encompassing embrace of all of us. He does not just love those who love Him or those who serve Him. He also loves those who despise Him and who rebel against Him.

Note also that His love is not coercive. He will not compel the hearts and minds of His sheep. He will invite and entice. He will call out to us. He will stand at the door and knock. His arms will remain always outstretched to us. When we are lost, He will leave the flock to go and find us and invite us back. But He will not compel us.

Nor will He abdicate or delegate His responsibility for us as our primary caretaker. He alone is "the way, the truth, and the life." He alone atoned for all of our sins. He alone suffered on the cross and died for us, and He alone raised Himself from the dead on the third day for all of our sakes. He alone did this for each one of us, including you and each one of your children.

Bear in mind also that He invites parents and children alike to come unto Him as little children, meek and humble, willing to submit their wills to His, trusting that He is the Good Shepherd and that under His care there is never a need to fear. And He invites us to come unto Him in whatever forms of life we currently find ourselves. Thus, whether we are like the Pharisees, pointing our accusing fingers at the sinners, or if we are like the sinners, who cannot lift their eyes because of the shame and despair they feel, or if we are living a mix of both forms of life, He invites us to come unto Him in each of those places of pride and despair we pretend to occupy. At whatever level we currently occupy, His eyes are there, on an even level with our own, inviting us to His place of meekness and humility.

Think of all the ways your Savior loves you and cares for you, and then focus all your attention on His expression of that love, in the image of His face that you hold in your mind. Let that love inhabit your mind and your heart. Let it fill your body and your soul. Do not resist it or try to find a reason you do not deserve it. Just receive it and know that your God, your Shepherd, your Parent, loves you. Once you have done that, once you have let yourself receive His love, note what has happened to your fear and anxiety and worry. In that moment in which you accept that you are acceptable to God and you let His love in and allow it to fill you, you cannot simultaneously feel fear. His perfect love has, as John stated, cast out the fear. It is gone. It may come back, to be sure, but in that moment in which you were filled with charity, fear was nowhere to be found. Charity and fear cannot be together in a person's heart and mind simultaneously.

Finally, as the last step in this brief exercise, take a moment to think about your children and what it would feel like for them to be free of fear because it has been cast out by the perfect love of God. Just as the burden of your worry was lifted for those moments in which you were bathed in the glow of charity, so, too, can your children experience love instead of fear, hope instead of despair, and faith instead of a desire for control. This is the greatest gift you can give to your children, and it should be the greatest parental desire of your heart. You give this gift to your children after you have first received it from God.

So, your primary parental responsibility, above all others, is to accept the love of God into your heart and mind, as often and for as long of a time period as you can, and then to share it with your children. They will learn to recognize their Shepherd and hear His voice through their experience of His love in you. And then, if they, too, will accept His invitation to come unto Him and become yoked together with the Savior, on His level, they will be filled with His love and it will emanate from your children's hearts. At that time and in that moment, your family will, indeed, be perfect.

Conclusion

Perfect parents know full well that they are flawed, that they have committed sins against their children, and that they will do so again. Like the woman caught in adultery, they know they are guilty before the Law, and they know that they deserve the harsh punishment affixed to that sin. But it is not the Law that kneels next to them and extends a hand of mercy and forgiveness to them. It is the Lawgiver, the Lawmaker, the living Law who has lowered Himself to their level, whose gaze meets theirs, and who seeks not to condemn but to lift and uplift them with His love. No, there is nothing flawless about a perfect parent. On the contrary, as with individuals and spouses, parents' flaws and their faults, their infirmities and their sins, their weaknesses and disabilities, allow the Healer's balm into their souls. Frailty and weakness are like pores on parents' skin that will soak up the "Son" light and illuminate their hearts and minds with His grace and mercy. If we will hear His voice, and as His sheep submit our will and our trust to Him, letting His light and love parent our children, then all fear will depart from us, and we will be perfect parents, level with Christ and our children and full of His love.

CHAPTER 6

"The Perfecting of the Saints"

No man is an island, entire of itself. Every man is a piece of the continent, a part of the main.

—*John Donne*

The language of perfectionism, with its central schema of individual flawlessness, affects everything we think, feel, and do. It can even impact our understanding of the words we commonly read and share with each other in our primary language of communication. For example, Christ's commandment to be perfect in Matthew 5:48 is often read by English speakers as if it was given to individuals who are to each make themselves flawless. But, in fact, the commandment was given to a collective, to a group of people listening together to Christ teach His Sermon on the Mount. This means that Christ used the second person plural, not the second person singular, when He addressed His audience. If you were to read this verse in other languages, which use different words for the singular and plural forms of "you," like Spanish or German, it would be much easier to see this distinction and to confirm that this commandment to be perfect was given to the plural you. Perhaps if we English speakers followed the approach used by my friends here in the South, who might translate Christ's commandment as "be y'all perfect, even as y'all's Father which is in heaven is perfect," we would not fall prey to this error and we would embrace the concept of a collective perfection.

Even acknowledging that Christ spoke to the plural "you" when He gave the commandment to be perfect does not fully resolve the confusion of this passage, for one still might ask, "How can a group of people be perfect, even as God is perfect, when God is one and a group is many? In his letter to the fledgling Christian congregation in Ephesus, Paul explains exactly how this is done. He teaches that when we come together as "fellow citizens...of the household God" (Ephesians 2:19), sharing in one faith and one baptism, yet having different talents, gifts, and abilities, then just as the different parts of the body work together to constitute a single person, so, too, do the many different members of a congregation "fitly joined together" (Ephesians 4:16) constitute the body of Christ. And it is that body, consisting of the many that are one in faith, with Christ at its head, that can receive and emanate the perfect love of God and be therefore perfect even as our Father which is in heaven is perfect. In Paul's words, "we all come in the unity of the faith, and of the knowledge of the Son of God, unto a perfect man, unto the measure of the stature of the fulness of Christ" (Ephesians 4:13). By ourselves, we fall short of the glory of God, but together, unified in faith and submitting to our Savior as our head, we can all be raised by Him to His stature, and we can love with His love, and as a result, we can and will become for that time a perfect, collective corpus.

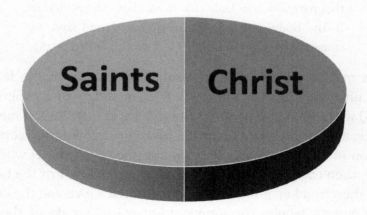

In this sense, the translation of the word *perfect* as whole, complete, and finished is right on target. We are whole, complete, and finished when, as Paul taught, all the members of the "whole body fitly joined together and compacted by that which every joint supplieth, according to the effectual working in the measure of every part, maketh increase of the body unto the edifying of itself in love" (Ephesians 4:16 KJV). Note that Paul, this beloved apostle of the Lord, makes no mention of individual flawlessness, and note also that the guiding telos, or purpose, for the body of Christ is not to rid itself of weakness or infirmity, but to build itself up in love. Such edification is only possible if the body is infused with Christ's love, which enters the body of Christ at its points of weakness and infirmity. As Paul taught the Corinthian saints:

> Much more those members of the body, which seem to be more feeble, are necessary: And those members of the body, which we think to be less honourable, upon these we bestow more abundant honour; and our uncomely parts have more abundant comeliness. For our comely parts have no need: but God hath tempered the body together, having given more abundant honour to

that part which lacked: That there should be no schism in the body; but that the members should have the same care one for another" (1 Corinthians12:22–25).

It makes sense to give more abundant honor to the feeble and uncomely parts of the body (i.e., members of a congregation) when we realize that it is through them that Christ's mercy, grace, and healing light enter the body and build up the congregation in love. And since there is not one of us who is without flaw, then each of us is a feeble and uncomely part of the body, and thereby a key point of access for Christ's love and the edification of the whole. The abundant honor Paul speaks of, then, is bestowed upon you!

Imperfect Saints

Denying Your Part in the Body of Christ

As we examine Paul's letter to the Corinthians more closely, we see how contrary his collective "perfect man" who is edified by God's love is to the individual flawlessness of perfectionism. In chapter 12, verses 14 through 20, Paul teaches the saints at Corinth that the body of Christ is not one member but many, and each body part is different and must be different in order for the whole to be complete and functional. He notes how absurd it would be if the foot were to deny its membership in the body simply because it was a foot and not the hand, or if the ear were to deny its critical role in the body because it was not the eye.

"My Church Assignment Is Not Significant."

As foolish as such a notion is when we think of the physical body and the obvious importance of all of its parts, we can easily buy in to this idea when we think of the body of Christ. It is actually quite common for a congregant to look at his or her seemingly less important role in the group as inconsequential and to secretly or sometimes openly complain that he or she does not have a more significant position. When your assignment at church is handing out hymnals each Sunday or passing the donation tray to the members, you may feel less useful or valuable than the deacons, the church elders, or the pastor. You may think your place in the body of Christ is expendable. It may feel like you are not a necessary part of the whole. When you entertain such thoughts and feelings, however, you risk making the body of Christ imperfect.

You also conflate an assignment in the Church with one's role in the body of Christ. An assignment to pass out hymnals or to be a pastor does not define the boundaries of a person's part in edifying the body of Christ alone. Not even close. Beyond your assignment, whatever it may be, you possess gifts and talents that are uniquely yours and that can help you serve and uplift others in a myriad of important and loving ways. No assignment is needed to visit a sick parishioner and offer him or her support, or to volunteer at a soup kitchen, or to witness to the divinity of Christ to your friends and other people you meet. It is up to you to evaluate your spiritual gifts and to discern how you can best apply them in the service of the whole. But your gifts and talents, too, do not exhaust all the ways you can edify the body of Christ. Remember, it is also your infirmity and weakness that is key to the perfection of the whole, for it is your feebleness that allows the healing balm of His love into the collective body of His saints.

"I Am Beneath Others."

Second, when you downplay your potential contribution to the body of Christ, you are embracing an unlevel view of its members. The foot is an apt analogy for this point because it is positioned at the bottom of the body when we are standing, sitting, or walking, and it must necessarily look upward to the other parts of the body, like the hand. It is also the farthest removed from the head. Similarly, it is easy for us to think that other members of our church congregation are somehow elevated above us and have received more "significant" assignments or an elevated status because they are better than we are, or worthier.

Such thinking might make sense in other types of corporations, like a business that is hierarchically organized according to things like educational degrees and one's ability to generate a profit, but it has no place in the context of the Christian corpus. For we must never forget that the One who is the head of the body of the saints abased Himself and willingly occupied the role of the least comely and least honored parts of the body, so He could succor each of us as one of us. He supped with the publicans, walked among the sinners, and knelt beside the dirty, the lame, and the maimed. By so doing, He demolished any concept of hierarchy and taught that the greatest of us is the least among us and the least of us is the greatest.

I recall a poem that helped me learn this significant lesson when I was struggling with what I thought at the time was a lowly position of no value or significance in my church. It is titled "Too Small?" (1935) and its author is unknown. It reads:

> Father, where shall I work today'
> And my love flowed warm and free.
> Then He pointed me out a tiny spot,
> And said, "Tend that for Me."
> I answered quickly, "Oh, no, not that.
> Why, no one would ever see,
> No matter how well my work was done.
>
> Not that little place for me!"
> And the word He spoke, it was not stern,
> He answered me tenderly,
> "Ah, little one, search that heart of thine;
> Art thou working for them or Me?
> Nazareth was a little place,
> And so was Galilee."

"My Small Part in the Whole Doesn't Make a Difference."

A third issue with this way of thinking is that the individual who questions the value of his or her role is focused on the part, on the self, and not the whole, not on the body of Christ. This is a problem, not only because it is self-centered, but also because it is impossible for us in our limited and partial view of things to appreciate how exactly "the effectual working in the measure of every part maketh increase of the body unto the edifying of itself in love" (Ephesians 4:16 kjv). Consider a cell in your physical body, let's say a single neuron located in your foot. Even the most expert biochemist cannot tell you all the ways this one cell in the body participates in and contributes to your thoughts, feelings, and activities. Indeed, it is often only when something goes wrong with that neuron that we gain insight into its important role in the body's functioning.

Similarly, no member can fully understand or appreciate the significance of his or her unique role in edifying the body of Christ in love. Christ alone can trace the effects of our yoked labor alongside Him to the perfection of His body. A kind word here and a smile there, even as we hand out a hymnal or the donation tray to a fellow congregant, may seem like nothing to us, but it could mean something important to someone else. And if you were not there doing your part, no matter its size or seeming importance, then the body of Christ would be the lesser for it.

I have a diary from when I was six years old with an entry I wrote following the funeral of a kind old man from church whom I had nicknamed the "Candy Man." I remember this man clearly to this day. Every Sunday he would bring hard candy to church in his coat pockets, and he would hand the candy out to the kids until he ran out of it. In my journal entry, at age six, mind you, I wrote about how much I loved the candy man and how kind he was to me, and it was not just because I like candy. He genuinely touched my heart. His was a small act that few people noticed or cared about at the time (much like the birth of a baby boy in a manger over two thousand years ago), but I noticed it, and it made going to church every Sunday more of a joy for me. When he died, I was so sad. I missed him and did not look forward to going to church quite as much as before. The body of Christ, though still full of love and well-edified, was ever so slightly less than it had been before, now that my friend, the candy man, was no longer a part of it. John Donne's poem that starts this chapter comes back to mind. The poem continues:

> If a clod be washed away by the sea,
> Europe is the less.
> As well as if a promontory were.
> As well as if a manor of thy friend's
> Or of thine own were:
> Any man's death diminishes me,
> Because I am involved in mankind,
> And therefore never send to know for whom the bell
> tolls;
> It tolls for thee.

No matter how small your role, no matter how feeble you may be and less honorable or uncomely you may feel, no matter how many sins you have committed, no matter your flaws and errors, you are an invaluable part of the perfect collective "man" that is the body of Christ. And with Paul we proclaim that more abundant honor and comeliness is bestowed upon you, not in spite of all those weaknesses and infirmities of body and spirit, but precisely because of them, because you are a precious access point for Christ's grace and mercy, a pore in the body through which His light can enter and fill the entire body with more of His pure divine love. You are an essential part of the perfection that Christ commands of us all.

Denying Others' Part in the Body of Christ

Congregants tend not only to question the value of their own roles in the body of Christ. Some also judge the worth of their peers in contributing to the whole. Sadly, we have heard people say that certain members are not contributing to the good of the church. They see them as a drag on the congregation and a barrier to its well-being. Some go so far as to say that some members should not even come to church until they can get their lives together or until they can get their kids to be more reverent and less distracting during worship services.

When we feel this way, the message of our judgmental verbal and nonverbal communication comes through to others loud and clear: "You are welcome, once you overcome your weaknesses, reduce your flaws, and at least appear to be faultless. However, right now we have no need of you in your current feeble and uncomely state." When members judge and ostracize others in this way, it is as Paul notes, as absurd as the eye telling the hand, "I have no need of thee," or the head saying to the foot, "I have no need of you" (1 Corinthians 12:21). Of course, the eye absolutely needs the hand and the head depends upon the foot, no matter how dirty, withered, or ugly each may be. All the parts are needed and essential.

When we put down another member of our congregation, either out loud in direct confrontation or in gossip behind their back or by a dirty or unkind look, or even in our own minds, we make ourselves uneven with the parts of the body of Christ, including its head. We pretend as if we are a more important, more valuable member of the body than others, and by doing so we puff ourselves up, demean others, and deny the love of Christ extended to us in His meekness and humility. We break what we think might be a viable candidate for an eleventh commandment: Thou shalt not compare!

The Sin of Comparison

Why do we compare to others? Recall from chapter 2 that the language of perfectionism is imbued with comparison. First, we compare ourselves to the metaphysical ideal of flawlessness. Once we realize that we all fall short of that abstract ideal, we focus on excellence, on trying to approximate the ideal in the best possible way. As we do that, we cannot help but see who around us appears more excellent and less excellent, and we inevitably draw comparisons between their apparent excellence in modeling the ideal and our own. The Pharisees and scribes are the quintessential comparers. They know they cannot be flawless, but they sure can be more excellent keepers of the Law than the sinners around them, and in that comparison, they find some brief solace, some temporary respite from the gnawing, haunting truth that tantalizes them, the truth that the flawlessness they really crave always remains just beyond their reach.

On the other side, acknowledged and obvious sinners, like the woman whom the Pharisees caught in adultery or the alcoholic sitting next to you in church whose breath reeks of alcohol, also compare. They know they have fallen completely short of the ideal of flawlessness and they know they are not approximating that ideal with any degree of excellence. When they look at others who appear not to struggle as they do, they see them as worthier, more self-disciplined, more deserving of God's love. They also accept the judgments of the apparently more excellent people, like the Pharisees, who condemn them. Why wouldn't they? They think, "They must be right. I am a failure. Everyone can see my sins. Everyone knows that I am lost."

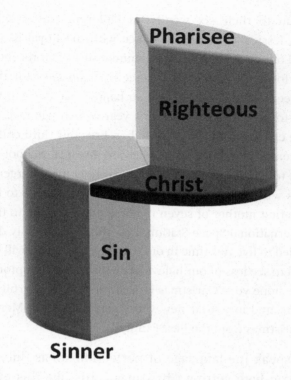

Most of us compare in both these directions at the same time and even in relation to the same people at the same time. That is, we can be puffed up in judgment of some church members who seem to sin or fail more than we do, and simultaneously we feel ashamed of how far we fall behind other seemingly more righteous congregational peers. Think, for example, of Christmastime and the feelings you have when you read through cards you receive from family and friends at that time of year. Perhaps you have received a card somewhat like this one:

> Greetings from the Best Family and Happy Holidays!
> David, our oldest, or you may know him as Senator
> Best, continues his work on Capitol Hill for our won-
> derful state. His wife, Jennifer, focuses on her charity
> work with cancer survivors and is kept busy being a

mom to their six wonderful children. Our daughter, Jessica, continues to dance with the Royal Ballet
in London and loves every minute of it. She recently
performed a solo performance of *Swan Lake* for the
Queen of England. We are so happy that she will be
performing in New York this year, which will give us
the chance to fly out and see her. Eric, our third child,
recently graduated from Harvard Medical School at
the top of his class and will specialize in neurosurgery.
His wife, Elizabeth, is still on track with NASA to be
the first mother of seven to complete a mission to the
International Space Station. Dad and I have finally decided to live full-time in our Tuscany home and will be
sad to see less of our beloved friends in the Hamptons.
We hope your Christmas is as white and wonderful as
ours, and may your new year be as successful. Merry
Christmas from the Best Family!

If you speak the language of perfectionism as fluently as we
do, then you hate getting Christmas cards like this every year,
because you find yourself feeling a mix of self-loathing and self-
righteousness as you read each line. Clearly, the Best family
is more excellent than your family is, and as you consider the
distance in excellence between them and you, it hurts you and
makes you sad. At the same time, you wonder, *Who sends out a
card like this? What braggards! What lack of couth! They are so full
of themselves. Who do they think they are?* This is the essence of
envy: We want to be like them, and yet we despise them for their
apparent excellence at the same time. And through it all, nothing
between us and them is even and level.

The Best family may have done their part to make themselves
uneven with us and others, but in our comparison and jealousy,
we have pressed ourselves below them and above them simultaneously. More importantly, by comparing, we have become

unlevel with Christ, who remains always meek and lowly of heart, and who invites us and the Best family to join Him there. Ultimately, the consequence is that the members of the body of Christ are not "tempered" (1 Corinthians 12:24) by Him and are not "jointly fitted" (Ephesians 4:16). As a result, His love is diminished, and the light of the body is dimmed.

An Abhorrence for Dependency

Why do we do this? Why do we lift ourselves up above others and act as if their role in our congregation is less valuable than our own, while simultaneously lowering ourselves beneath other congregants, telling ourselves we are less than them? Why can't everyone accept each other and feel like they belong, and how can we help each other realize that all the parts of the body of Christ are essential to perfection? One source of our resistance to level and "jointly fitted" wholeness can be found in our desire to be independent and self-sufficient, a desire that is deeply embedded in the perfectionist's psyche and strongly reinforced by our individualistic culture. Indeed, Paul's teaching on corporate perfection can be particularly hard for many Americans to accept, because it requires submission, integration into a larger whole, and dependency on others. For many Americans, the values we prize include the freedom to exercise our individual wills, demonstrating our uniqueness, and living in such a way that we do not have to depend upon others.

Perfectionists abhor dependence, because it entangles us in other people's lives and problems in a way that our or their mistakes and failings can get us and/or them hurt. When I think of the risks of dependency, I think of sitting in the passenger seat of the car with each of my children as they learned how to drive. It is genuinely frightening to put your safety and the well-being of all of the passengers in your car in the hands of fifteen-year-old kids! They could literally get you all killed! You tense up, your heart rate accelerates, and you find yourself instinctively pressing your foot down on the floorboard of the car as if a brake pedal was there and you could somehow magically stop the car and save yourself, your child, other drivers on the road, and the vehicle. You find yourself wondering, as you press your foot down ever harder and your life passes before your eyes, why you agreed to have children in the first place. If you knew how strongly they would affect you and your mental, emotional, and physical health, and not just in the car, but in all aspects of your life, you might never have agreed to submit yourself to such entanglements and dependency. It can feel like their dependency upon you has taken you and your life hostage!

But children are one thing. They are bound to you by blood and genes and an ethical, spiritual, and legal stewardship. Fellow congregants, on the other hand, are the people you see on Sundays and maybe occasionally on other days of the week. Your relationship to them is mostly a product of your church membership and the fact that you choose to gather to worship in the same building once a week. Sharing obligations with them and having to depend upon them ought to happen only to the degree that you want it to happen, and it should never get too messy and too involved. Ideally, we would decide just how much to depend on others in our congregations, and we would keep it to a minimum.

Chasing the Ideal of Independence

As we have already mentioned, dependence can be especially challenging for Americans. After all, it is independence that typifies us, in part because we emerged from our status as colonies into a full-fledged country by fighting and, in many cases, dying for independence from the British Empire and for the right to govern ourselves. And since then we have continued to fight and die in defense of these freedoms for ourselves and for others throughout the world. Thus, it is of deep, deep importance to us, collectively and individually, that we are not beholden to anyone and that no one else controls our destiny. Thus, for many

Americans, dependency is looked upon as a kind of disorder and is used as a truly dirty word.

And it is not just having independence that we value. The manner in which we Americans gain the autonomy we desire is almost as important to us as the autonomy itself. The American dream is one in which any one of us, regardless of circumstance, can and should, by the power of our own indomitable will and through the exercise of our unique strengths (e.g., our individual talents and gifts), pull ourselves up by our bootstraps, and become all that we want to be. The self-made man or woman is our ambition. The ideal American is a person who carves him- or herself out of obscurity and achieves greatness without help from an inheritance, a trust fund, or government aid.

Perhaps this is one of the reasons so many of us admire Abraham Lincoln. Dirt poor, from the lower class, and lacking in educational opportunities and resources, he found his own way out of his impoverished circumstances, mostly educating himself, reading by candlelight every night, and ultimately willing himself into the greatest office of this country—and into becoming one of the greatest presidents we have ever had. His story resonates with the ideal manner in which each of us seeks self-sufficient success. Lincoln is the quintessential self-made person we aspire to be. He is an excellent model of the ideal of independence.

Being independent and gaining that independence in the right way, the self-made way, matters deeply to us, but we are just as concerned with promoting the autonomy and self-reliance of others, especially our children. Indeed, we mark the point at which our children have become fully functioning, mature adults and contributing members of society when they are able to live on their own and do not need us, their parents, or other social services and safety nets to meet their material needs. When children cannot make it on their own, then something is wrong, not only with the child, but perhaps also with the parents, who apparently did not properly raise their kids to be self-reliant citizens.

Maybe the parents were not tough enough, and as a result their kids have grown up soft, weak, and feeble instead of strong and capable. Certainly, a number of parents and their peers wonder about such parental missteps when their children fail to launch successfully into an independent or at least mostly independent adulthood.

Running Away from Inferiority

It is interesting that we place so much emphasis on self-sufficiency and strength, given that of all the creatures born into this world, human beings start out as the most dependent and weakest of almost any species, and we remain in that condition for a longer period of time than any other animal. A baby sea turtle will hatch alone on the seashore and immediately make its way to the ocean; it will live from then on without any need for caretaking. A foal can walk within hours of birth. A baby tiger can hunt for food on its own by eighteen months. And even a chimpanzee, our closest genetic relative, can survive on its own by age six. Human beings need much more than hours, days, weeks, months, or even a half dozen years to survive and function on their own. Some of you who have adult children still living at home with you may wonder whether there is any age at which your children could survive without your care!

Autonomy, self-reliance, and independence—these achievements are not a *fait accompli* for human beings. They are not simply a natural consequence of maturation, and they are not the defining characteristics of our natural, original state. Some of us—indeed, even many of us—might not become measurably self-sufficient in this life, and few of us, if we do accomplish some measure of autonomy, will be able to remain that way into our old age, and that is a scary thought for people who prize autonomy so strongly.

Our lack of inherent self-sufficiency is not only scary, but it can be intimidating when we look around at our supposedly less-advanced peers in other species and see how much more successful these other animals are in getting their young to the point of self-sufficiency than we are. Indeed, it can give us a kind of species-level inferiority complex! Psychoanalysts contend that an inferiority complex develops on a mostly unconscious level, when we fall short in achieving some aspect of our life that is important to us. If, for example, I had grown up in a family in which everyone, even the women, were almost seven feet tall, and I am not even six feet tall myself, then I might develop a kind of complex about being short. I might become schematic for height, and I might fixate on my diminutive stature, compared to my family, and blame my height for my failings, not just in sports, but in other aspects of my life. In other words, I will see my height as a flaw and a fault, an imperfection that is holding me back and bringing me down, keeping me from reaching my ideal self.

The thing about inferiority complexes is that when we experience the anguish of inferiority and all the failings that come with it, we are inclined to try to compensate for our lack. So, if I am the short one in my family, I may compensate by developing other physical abilities, like speed and agility. I may not be able to slam-dunk the basketball, but I can learn to dribble the ball down the court faster and more skillfully than my giraffe-like siblings. In other words, since I cannot will myself to be taller, I will find other ways to "measure up," and if I can do so successfully, then I will find a place and a role in my family, and I will be able to make my mark on the world and live my dreams just as successfully and self-reliantly as my siblings.

Overcompensation and the Superiority Complex

It is possible, however, if I experience my inferiority too painfully (e.g., the taller siblings relentlessly tease their shorter brother) and if my efforts to compensate for my inferiority fail, that I may overcompensate. That is, I may develop a superiority complex in which I seek not only to measure up to others, but I seek to measure myself above others, and ideally above all others. If I can pretend I am superior, then I can hide from others and from myself my true feelings of inadequacy, my fear of failure, and my lack of confidence in myself. Some view Napoleon as an example of overcompensation and the superiority complex (Adler, 1927), probably because he proclaimed himself to be a "superior being" and because he crowned himself the emperor of France to prove it!

Perhaps, as a species, human beings, or at least a number of us, have come to develop a kind of shared superiority complex in which we seek to overcompensate for the obvious inherent weakness and helplessness with which we are born. Perhaps we have become schematic for strength and independence because we so clearly lacked both of these things in our early lives. Being strong and self-sufficient then appears to us to be of supreme importance in what seems to us to be an obviously dog-eat-dog world. It is the weakest wildebeest, after all, who falls behind as the herd runs away from the lioness and gets eaten. If asked what kind of animal you want to be like, no one says a wildebeest—and certainly not the weakest of the wildebeests! The whole wildebeest species appears to us as weak, and we want nothing to do with that. Instead, we want to be like lions and eagles and bears. These are the emblems on our flags and signets, and we place them there to demonstrate our superior strength and self-sufficiency to the world. Perhaps we prop up strength so no one, including ourselves, will see our inherent original weakness.

This form of overcompensation was perhaps most infamously exemplified by the Nazi Party. After the humiliating defeat of Germany in the First World War had exposed Germany's fragility and weakness to the German people and the world the Nazis initiated a political and military campaign founded upon the premise of racial superiority and the promise of a renewed, invincible Fatherland. Of course, in order to lift one race up, other races had to be put down. The Nazis quickly generated propaganda, blaming the Jews for the loss of the war and promising that a Germany cleansed of Jews and other inferior people (e.g., the disabled and "Gypsies") would be free of the weakness and frailty that had hindered Germany's greatness and dominance in the world in the past. In their endeavor to prove this point to themselves and the world, the Nazis conducted a program of genocide the likes of which the world had never seen before, ultimately initiating a Second World War that resulted in the deaths of tens of millions of people.

Surely, church congregations are far removed from the Nazis, but they are not immune to overcompensation, superiority complexes, and scapegoating. Few members are comfortable having their frailty exposed to others, and some members, in an effort to avoid that exposure, do try to overcompensate for feelings of inadequacy, unworthiness, and inferiority by propping up the veneer of righteousness and assuming a superior stance over other members, often in the form of judgment, gossip, and criticism. Moreover, those whose sins are not easily hidden or who deviate in appearance and/or action from the stereotype of a Christian disciple are sometimes scapegoated and ostracized from the group. It would seem that even though we know that all have fallen short of God's glory (Romans 3:23) and that all of us, like sheep, have gone astray (Isaiah 53:6), and even though Christ invites us to come unto Him in our frailty and sinfulness and fallenness, the language of perfectionism and the cultural support it receives can lead us to resist any exposure of weakness and dependency upon each other as we seek for the overcompensating appearance of individual righteousness and self-sufficiency.

Perfect Saints

The Way of Weakness

The contrast between overcompensation, superiority complexes, and scapegoating, and the manner of living exemplified by our God, is undeniable. Our God, who, as we discussed in chapter 3, is all-knowing, all-powerful, and as strong and flawless as can be, willingly chose to enter our world exactly as we do, not as a lion, but as a lamb, fully dependent on His parents for everything and completely frail and helpless. There can be no doubt that Christ, instead of choosing the path of strength, walked the way of weakness, submitting Himself to flawed parents who would make mistakes in raising Him and integrating Himself into a family, a language, and a culture that, like any worldly context, is inevitably filled with errors and shortcomings. Indeed, He allowed Himself to depend upon others at every step of His life.

During His three-year mission, Christ was homeless and jobless. He relied on others for meals and for raiment and for a bed and a roof over His head. He even let others decide His fate at His trial and submitted to the manner of death others chose for Him. He did not even have His own burial plot, but He had to borrow one from a friend. We have already noted in chapter 3 that when the devil tempted Him to exercise His strength over the elements, over the heavens, and over people, even as He was exhausted from a forty-day fast, He refrained from flexing His divine muscle and remained meek and lowly still. When the soldiers whipped Him and placed a crown of thorns upon His head mockingly, He allowed it and He endured it without fighting back in any degree. Through it all, with every temptation to manifest His divinity through strength, He continued to walk the way of weakness, and He did so from the moment of His birth up to the final anguishing moment of His death.

Why did He do this, and what does His walk of weakness mean for us? At the very least, it means that rather than despising the original frailty with which we were born, we must seek to become as little children. We must reject the temptation to over-compensate for our weakness and frailty. We must learn to accept and even embrace our natural, original state of dependency and feebleness. This does not mean that we simply accept dependency for dependency's sake or embrace an abstract concept of pacifism. No, it means that we accept our dependency on Christ and upon each other as "fellow-citizens" (Ephesians 2:19) in the body of Christ. We walk the way of weakness for His sake, knowing that it is only through our weakness that our Lord and His love can have access to us and thereby to the body as a whole.

What does this mean in practical terms? It means that when someone offends us, we focus on Christ instead of the offender, and we forgive them for His sake and owing to His mercy and meekness, not our own. As Christ described it, walking in His way means that if someone compels us to walk a mile with them, we walk two miles with them. It means that if someone hits us upon the cheek, we offer them our other cheek. It means that we live as lambs and not as lions, that we live as little children, human children, who are incapable of survival by ourselves and who must depend on others, even similarly frail others, for our survival, for our spiritual survival. It means accepting that God created us in a state of dependence, not so that we would grow out of it, but so that we would accept and live into our dependence upon Him alongside and with each other. It means that the corporate perfection God commands of us is something altogether different from flawlessness, strength, and independence.

Conclusion

When together we recognize as congregations what Christ so clearly demonstrated in His walk of weakness and taught to His disciples, which is that "My grace is sufficient for thee: for my strength is made perfect in weakness," then we, like Paul will jubilantly proclaim together, "Most gladly therefore will I rather glory in my infirmities, that the power of Christ may rest upon me" (2 Corinthians 12:9). For if Paul glories in his infirmities because those infirmities are the access points for the grace of the Lord, then so, too ought we, the corporate body of Christ, gathered together in our congregations wherever they may be, be glad for and glory in our shared infirmities and dependency on each other and our God. We should bestow more abundant honor upon our feebler parts, for we know it is through the wounded and the sick that His healing balm can enter the body and heal us all together.

If any of us feels inadequate to the body and the members around us, we must avoid all temptation to overcompensate by proving our strength and superiority, for we will elevate ourselves right out of balance with our Savior, who is meek and lowly of heart and who seeks us in our weakness. We must likewise avoid the temptation to remove ourselves from the body, believing our part in it to be of little or no value or use, for there again we create an imbalance with the Savior and act as if we know better than He does what parts of the body are needed for perfection. This is not His way. He does not seek flawlessness in His body. He seeks for weakness, for infirmity, for sin, for it is there where He can heal us with His mercy. It is there where He can actualize His grace. It is there where His love and His light can be given and received. It is there in His way, the way of weakness, where perfection is truly possible.

CHAPTER 7

A Perfect World?

Then it was as if I suddenly saw the secret beauty of their hearts, the depths of their hearts where neither sin nor desire nor self-knowledge can reach, the core of their reality, the person that each one is in God's eyes. If only they could all see themselves as they really are. If only we could see each other that way all the time. There would be no more war, no more hatred, no more cruelty, no more greed. I suppose the big problem would be that we would fall down and worship each other.

—Thomas Merton

At this point, we have covered a number of key points concerning the perfection Christ commands of us, which are summarized below:

- The perfection commanded of us by Christ is not a quality or characteristic of an individual, like flawlessness or independence. It is a way of relating to others that is enabled by God's way of relating to us. God relates to all of His children through His love, and He does so evenly, allowing His love, like the rain and the sunshine to fall on the just and the unjust, on both His friends and His enemies alike.

- God's love enters this world and falls upon all of us in its fully divine and heavenly illuminated brilliance through Jesus Christ, who is literally the embodiment of God's love. As God's only begotten Son, fully human and fully divine, Christ alone can bring God's love into our world and share it with each of us. But He does not do this from an elevated position. He does this as one of us, even the weakest among us, kneeling right there beside us with His eyes meeting our own, so He can succor us in our weakness and infirmity.

- The first step we take in obeying Christ's commandment to be perfect, even as our Father who is in heaven is perfect, is to accept Christ's embrace in our weakness, to come unto Him in our infirmity and fragility, take His yoke (i.e., His love) upon us, and submit ourselves to Him, as would a little child.

- Once yoked to Christ, we carry together His easy burden, which is His love, and with Him we extend His love out into the world. We practice this extension of His love most often and most directly with our partners and with our children, seeking to remain even with Christ and with each other in our weakness and complete dependence upon Christ for His love and light.

- Perfection is a commandment given to the plural "ye" that cannot be achieved without the feeble and less honorable parts of the whole, including when we ourselves are those feeble and less honorable parts. A plurally perfected people know that it is those members who are weak, frail, and infirm, upon whom we ought to bestow the greatest honor, for they/we are the pores through which the love of God enters the body of Christ and thereby perfects it.

- In all of these relationships, we must remind ourselves and accept the reality that the love of God will not always abide in us, because of the unevenness we create with others and our Savior. However, this is not a cause for despair, but as with Paul, it gives us reason to rejoice, for the unevenness that results from our sins, our infirmities, our flaws, and our faults provides us with an opportunity to practice repentance and forgiveness with each other and with Christ. And, when we repent and forgive each other and accept the forgiveness of our Lord, then we again become level with Christ and with each other, and we regain our access to His godly love. Once again His love emanates outward through us into all our relationships.

Now, as we conclude this book, there is one final key feature of the perfection Christ commanded of us that needs to be addressed:

- When we state that in those moments when we keep God's commandment to be perfect His love will emanate from us into "all our relationships," we do mean all of them, including our relationships with people unseen, with people who do not know us or care about us, and even with people who might want to hurt us. The love of God is no respecter of persons, and so, too, when we love with the love of God, we will love all people, even the people who "despitefully use" (Matthew 5:44) us. The love of God, then, bestowed upon us when we are yoked to Christ can make the world even, complete, and whole. Indeed, it can, for that time, perfect the world.

In a Perfect World, All Relationships Are Even

The achievement of a perfect world, even if it is gained for only a moment, requires that all relationships are even with each other at the level of Christ's humility and meekness. The diagram below shows all of the participants in the relationships of life that we have reviewed in this book, from the individual to the world. In a perfect world, we would place this diagram on its side and no entity represented by a sphere would be above or below any other. We could run our finger over the borders of each circle and feel no difference in depth or height.

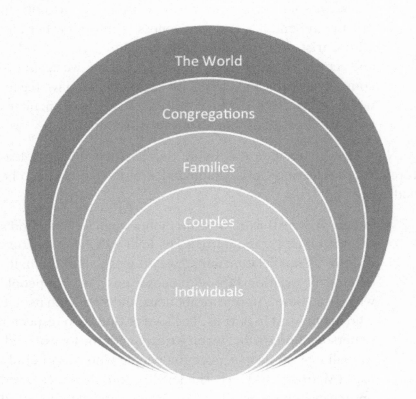

Even Religions Must Be Even

It may come as a surprise to you for us to say that one of the chief threats to the evenness of a perfect world actually comes from within institutions of faith. Churches are supposed to be carriers of God's love and emblems of His light and grace, and in so many wonderful cases they are. However, many churches also teach their members and publicly proclaim that their faith tradition is true and that other religious traditions are false. From this perspective they might ask, how can we be level or why would we want to be level when other churches are wrong and our church is right? Isn't our religion inherently above other faiths because of the truths we know or because of the special or chosen relationship our church has with God? Furthermore, if our church is the one true church, then wouldn't it also be closer to the ideal of perfection than other churches and institutions in the world? Isn't it in that Platonic sense, then, more excellent than other churches? Or, perhaps, if our church is chosen by God and led by Him, it is actually flawless and infallible, just as God is.

These questions and ideas have been raised by many people from a variety of different faith traditions over the course of history, and in many cases, the principles of perfectionism have been comfortably applied to the institution of the church itself. Concepts of papal, prophetic, scriptural, and spiritual infallibility can be found in Christianity, Islam, Judaism, and Hinduism, as is the notion of being chosen above all others. It would seem then, from at least some of these religious perspectives, that common people might not be capable of achieving flawlessness, but institutionalized religions, holy writ, and in special cases, the purified people who lead the church are.

But, no church has pulled off infallibility. A church cannot achieve infallibility any more than an individual can, because, as we discussed in chapter 2, flawlessness is not possible in this physical, changing world. Even a cursory review of any church's history will show that errors, mistakes, and outright prejudice, dogmatism, and truly bad behaviors have occurred. Unfortunately, the pretense of perfection has led many of these religious institutions to deny, ignore, and cover up these failings in order to maintain the appearance of flawlessness upon which they have predicated much of their credibility. From the perspective of perfection as love that is complete and even, this propping up of infallibility is not necessary, nor is it desirable, and it never lasts. It can only make a church more appealing to its members or those considering joining it for so long. Then, when a church's weaknesses and even sins are brought to light—and they always are—church members and the public at large will begin to question not only the credibility of the church, but sometimes also the existence and character of the God it claims to worship and who supposedly leads it.

Disillusioned, many people will leave the church and look for alternatives to organized religion, such as nontheistic spiritual traditions. And this reaction makes perfect sense. If congregants have based their commitment to their church on the belief that the church will never lead them astray or do anything wrong, and then it clearly does something wrong, then the members' commitment to the church will and should weaken. Seeing a church struggle in this way, other perfectionistic churches may cast judgments and accusations at the exposed church, raising themselves above it and ratcheting up their own efforts to avoid the exposure of their own flaws. In this way, the pretense of perfection only serves to create unevenness across churches. It also ultimately weakens the relationship of many people to God, and it hinders His work of perfection, or more precisely, the extension of His love to all people and institutions.

With a proper understanding of the perfection that Christ has commanded of us, we would think that even if a church and its leaders could somehow manage to be infallible and flawless, they would not want to be, because perfection of this flawless variety would negate the church's dependency on Christ and shut off its access points to receive His redeeming love. As such, a flawless-ness-minded church would not only elevate itself above other more obviously flawed churches, societal institutions, and even its own flawed members, it would inevitably also elevate itself above Christ, who does not join us individually or institutionally in our puffed-up pride and pretense of perfection, but seeks us in our weakness and humility.

We can see at this institutional level just how different the language of perfectionism is from the language of perfect love, and we can see how dominant the language of perfectionism is within religious institutions. Think about it. How many churches have you seen openly acknowledge and embrace institutional weakness and frailty? How many church leaders preach and practice institutional repentance? How many churches see and publicly acknowledge themselves as being just as weak and fallen as every other church before Christ and admit to being fully dependent upon His mercy and grace right alongside every other earthbound institution?

In a perfect world—meaning a world in which all persons and institutions are even before the Lord in their shortcomings, flaws, infirmities, and failures, a world in which we all recognize our dependence on Christ and we rejoice in our weakness because it provides the very access point for His love—every church would acknowledge and embrace their shared weakness and dependency on the Lord. There would be no propped-up flawlessness of any kind. Churches, like individuals, couples, families, and congregations, would practice repentance and seek forgiveness from God, knowing that with that forgiveness, love will enter the institution and emanate from it toward its members and toward other institutions, whether they be churches, governments, or businesses.

The members of a church whose leaders acknowledge and bring to Christ all of the church's failings, flaws, and even sins would love this repentant church more, not less than a flawless church, because the church would openly depend upon Christ, the Living Truth, and its members would be bound to the church by His love, not by a pretense of infallibility. The repentant church would be bathed in God's merciful forgiveness, and it would be in that forgiveness and in that redemption and in that grace that the love of God is poured out upon the institution and the institution is level and even with all other institutions, its own people, and its God. Only then, when at every level of relationship—from our individual and familial relationships with

Christ to the relationships of all churches to Christ—when we are level and even with Him and thereby with each other, is a perfect world possible.

Perfection Is Possible!

Perhaps you may think we are too hopeful, even naïve in our goal of a perfect world. The idea that God's love could extend from God through Christ to individuals and into our marriages and families and then also into our churches and then from our churches out into the world, seems like an obvious impossibility. Maybe we cannot keep Christ's commandment to be perfect, even as our Father who is in heaven is perfect, after all. We, the authors, might be tempted to agree with this sentiment as we look out at the world around us. We are therapists after all, and we deal regularly in relationships in which love of any sort can be hard to come by, let alone the love of God. We understand very well what we are up against, but two things give us comfort and give us hope.

Incremental Perfection

The first source of hope and comfort is that we ourselves have felt the love of God in the redeeming grace of Jesus Christ. He has reached out to us in our weakness and infirmity, and He has healed our hearts and shared His light and love with us. When He does that, we feel His love for our families, our congregations, and the world. This doesn't happen every day, and when it does happen it does not last all that long. Indeed, we quickly fall back into making ourselves uneven with Him and the people around us. Pride and despair have been frequent passengers on our journey through life, and we regularly feel both above others and beneath others at the same time. But despite all that, miraculously, we have felt His love for us. As undeserving as we may be, as flawed as we certainly are, we have felt His love, which means we have known for moments of time, perfection.

In our experience, we are most often even and filled with God's love when we acknowledge our sins and our failures and when we cry out for His mercy and redemption. We receive His love when we are vulnerable and sensitive and when we are not trying to be strong and independent. It comes in when we let our guard down just a bit and we stop trying to measure up or overcompensate. We experience it when we loosen our grip on doing everything right and we submit to Him, depend upon Him, and admit we need Him. In short, we are most likely to be perfect when we stop trying to be perfect.

It is then, right then, immediately in our vulnerability, when we give up on our own perfectionistic efforts, that we are perfected in His love. As we give ourselves over to the truth, to the Living Truth who is Christ, and acknowledge that we are just little children who are helpless, lost, and in need of His care; in that moment He meets us there, right in front of us, not above us or below us. His eyes meet ours. Like the woman caught in adultery, His hand takes our hand so gently, and it becomes clear to us that He has been waiting for us, standing at the door and knocking the whole time. He has been waiting ever so patiently for us to yield our will to His and to let Him in. It seems so easy at that moment. How did we ever forget that all it takes is the submission of our will to His? Why did we let so much time go by before turning to Him? We know it is right and we know it is true. In His embrace, we remember that this is where we belong. This is who we really are. This is perfection.

It does not last. It cannot last. The phone rings. The car in front of me cuts me off. My child comes in the room crying because her brother was mean to her—again. Something always comes along that interrupts the moments of perfect love. And just as immediately as the love came in, I unlevel myself. I find myself annoyed that someone would call at this late hour. Who does that? I am angry with the driver who cuts me off. Who does she think she is? She doesn't own the road. I am tired of my kids fighting and this child always tattling. Deal with it yourselves! You are old enough now. Work it out.

And then the love is gone, and I will remain out of perfect relationship for a while. I will forget how available Christ was and how easy it was to receive Him. Instead of yielding, I will try to steel myself against weakness so I can be strong enough to face the trials of my life. I will judge people around me so that I can feel justified about how I am doing by comparison, or I will become jealous because they seem to have an easier or fuller life than I do. I will speak again the language of perfectionism.

But just because perfection was short-lived and may not come around again for some time, that does not mean it was not real. In that moment of submission, brief though it was, I was loved with a divine love, and I, too, loved with a divine love. I loved my wife, my kids, my friends, my fellow church members, and even my enemies and strangers. I loved them all, and I loved them as Christ loved them, with His love and not my own, and in that moment my relationship with Christ and everyone else was perfect, level, whole, and complete. In that moment I spoke another language, the language of perfect love, and because that moment was real and did happen, I have become bilingual. I can speak the language of perfect love again. I can repent and obey Christ's commandment again.

Consider our experience an example of incremental perfection. When speaking the language of perfectionism, we are prone to all-or-nothing thinking. Either I am completely obedient and righteous or, if I commit the slightest error or sin, then I am completely disobedient and lost. This perfectionistic schema makes perfection, however we choose to define it, an overwhelming, impossible achievement. We are asking instead that you shift your thinking toward allowing yourself to feel God's love just ever so slightly more often in your life and letting it stay with you just a bit longer each time it comes. Think of this as a "baby steps" approach to perfection, if you like. A little more repentance here and a little more forgiveness there is all we ask, not flawless righteous living all the time. Open yourself up to God with vulnerability and dependence just slightly more today than you did yesterday. Practice opening the door He is knocking on just a little more often. When you fail do not get discouraged, but be grateful, for that failure is itself an opportunity to practice receiving the love of God in your heart. So, when today is less love-filled than yesterday, it is no big deal. Just acknowledge and embrace your weakness as an access point for Christ's mercy, and repent and give it a little try again tomorrow.

Incremental perfection reminds me of recently teaching my daughter to serve a volleyball overhand. When she first wanted to do this, she went to the service line and tried to serve the ball over the almost eight-foot-tall net thirty feet away. She tried and tried and fell short every time. I offered to help her, but she wanted to do it herself. Eventually, she got frustrated and went back to serving underhand. A day or so later, when she was more open to my help, I taught her the motions one goes through in order to serve overhand successfully. I also told her that she needed to build up her strength and that it would take practice and time.

Once I trained her on a basic overhand serve, I stood her just a few feet in front of the net and told her to serve the ball over the net. She looked at me like, "Come on, Dad, anyone can do that. The net is too close. It's too easy." I told her that if she could successfully serve the ball over the net from this position, then she could take a step back and try again. She easily served the ball over the net. I could see on her face that even though she thought the task was easy, she was relieved that she had succeeded. She saw that she could serve the ball overhand over the net, in principle.

Then, after she succeeded with her first serve, I had her take a step back and do it again. I could see she was feeling even better when the ball went over the net again. After the next step back, she mishit the ball and it failed to go over the net. "No problem, take a step forward and let's get that serve back over the net. Easy enough. Now step back again and try from there." She hit it really well the next time, it sailed over the net, and she felt good yet again.

On and on we went like this, stepping back sometimes, forward other times. Once or twice, she even served successfully from behind the service line. Her progress was incremental, allowing her to feel some success and helping her gauge where she needed more practice. Most importantly, I always let her step forward to the point that she could see again that she could in principle succeed at the task.

So it is with God's love. You probably cannot just embrace it and hold on to it forever with one big act of repentance or forgiveness or conversion that ensures you will never lose it again. Like most of us, you have had to start small and you have experienced some momentary successes that let you know that it is possible for you to relate to Christ in His love. These small successes, like my daughter's serve close to the net, help you to feel encouraged about the possibility of having God's love in your heart more often and for a longer duration.

The perfectionist in you may have discounted these moments of evenness and love in the past, telling you it only counted if you got it right all the time, once and for all. From that perspective, you are not really obeying the commandment until you always obey the commandment. Such a view will result in the tantalization we talked about in chapter 2. Like my daughter when she first tried to serve over the net overhand, you will only think and care about flawlessness, and you will keep reaching for flawlessness and it will keep eluding your grasp. And, like my daughter, it will discourage you; it will make you miserable. Then, you will want to give up on flawlessness, like Kate from chapter 1, or you will obsess over flawlessness, like the young mother with OCD from chapter 2.

The language of perfection sends a different message: Every time you feel the love of God, no matter how short it lasts and no matter how rarely you feel it, you are perfect. You are level and even with the Savior, and you are in that moment keeping Christ's commandment just as fully as you keep any commandment. And, as with any commandment, you will slip and you will sin and you will break it, and that is cause to rejoice, for you now have the opportunity to repent and to become again perfect with Him. Indeed, this is a unique feature of the commandment to be perfect compared to all other commandments. Any time you humbly repent and seek forgiveness for the breaking of any of God's commandments, you are keeping the commandment to be perfect, for you are humble and meek, open to and accepting Christ's atoning mercy and grace, and His love is entering into you and filling you with His light. You and He are, in that moment, perfect!

The Way of Weakness

Our second source of hope and comfort is that we know that weakness finds a way into our lives no matter how hard we try to resist it. To those who seek after access to divine love, we know that the constant presence of weakness in our lives provides an ever-present opportunity to come unto Christ. As everyday manifestations of weakness expose our vulnerabilities to ourselves, to our God, and to each other, the opportunity for grace and redemption is provided to us. As hard as many people work to prop up their strengths and not fail, we know that no individual, no family, and no institution can ultimately avoid the exposure of their frailty. Eventually, no matter how hard we resist, deny, or try to hide our flaws, we all find ourselves on the path of weakness.

From the perspective of perfectionism, as we mentioned at the opening of this book, the exposure of our vulnerabilities and flaws is the worst thing that can happen to us, and we will do almost anything to try to deny and hide our frailty. As we discussed in chapter 6, we will often overcompensate for our weakness by trying to prove by all means possible that we are actually strong and independent. In so doing, unfortunately, we, like the Pharisees of Christ's time, will often look around for someone worse off than we are to help us feel better about ourselves. Or we will find fault in the people who have witnessed our weakness, and we will turn on them and point out their faults to try to level them with us by bringing them down. If we can prove that they are no more flawless than we are, then maybe, just maybe, we can convince ourselves that "nobody's perfect" and it will be okay.

This is how the world often works, and it creates a lot of stress, contention, propping up of the appearance of perfection, and the putting down of others. But it does not have to be this way. We could practice an alternative approach, not every day all day, but true to our incremental perfection concept, we could try it out, here a little and there a little. The alternative, as we have discussed throughout the book, is to practice accepting and even occasionally embracing weakness, by recognizing that weaknesses and faults are access points for grace, evenness, and love.

Embrace Repentance and Forgiveness

For example, consider the next time your child does something dumb and creates trouble for you. If, in reprimanding the child, you go too far and you lose your temper and you yell at the child and say demeaning things, then instead of going into your room and slamming the door and telling yourself that the child needed to hear those things and that it is the child's fault you got angry, and that she is wrong, not you, you might try something different. You could leave your room and walk down the hall to your child's room, open the door, and say, "I lost my temper, and I said some mean things to you, and that was wrong, and I am sorry. I hope you can forgive me." Even if you choose not to do this, you can recognize that you could have done this, and that it may have been right and good to have done this. Just allowing yourself to admit that it is possible to acknowledge the weakness of your temper to your child, and that you could allow yourself to be vulnerable to your child and your God in a moment of repentance, would be an important step in learning the language of perfect love and becoming more capable of speaking it to your loved ones.

Opportunities for acknowledging weakness and for speaking, even if only rarely, the language of perfect love abound. It is not necessary to seek after weakness and frailty, for both will find us all the time and in all our relationships. When frailty does find you—and it always does—instead of immediately denying it, hiding it, or running away from it, try, ever so gently, to take advantage of this moment of weakness as an opportunity to become even with our Lord by practicing repentance. At the same time, when the weaknesses of others find you, and their mistakes and faults cause you suffering and pain—and they always do—rather than becoming embittered—because you, in speaking the language of perfectionism, can easily imagine how they could have made a better choice, a choice that did not injure you, a flawless choice—try to the extent you are able to see their offense, as painful as it may be, as an opportunity for you to practice forgiveness.

The other day, one of my children made a mistake that could have led to a minor disaster for our family. It was obvious that he deeply regretted his error, and true to the language of perfectionism that he has learned so well, he was already beating himself up for what he had done. Crying and racked with guilt, he said he was sorry multiple times. Rather than forgive him, I spoke to him perfectionistically, reminding him of how potentially damaging his mistake could have been and telling him all the measures he should have taken to make sure the error never even had a chance of occurring. Regrettably, I even recall saying that it was not enough to be sorry and that he simply could never make that kind of mistake because it could be too devastating. He had to take all precautions and he had to do everything right and he could never get it wrong.

What good could my comments have done? The event had already passed. The mistake was already made, the disaster was averted, luckily, and he already felt as awful as possible. Even if disaster had resulted, there could be no magical Superman-like reversal of time. What could any of my perfectionistic rhetoric possibly have achieved? I know what I wanted it to achieve. I wanted to completely control things in the future so that my fear of this disaster would never be realized. I wanted my son to be flawless in this one thing so that I could feel secure and less anxious about it.

But what did I get? I passed on all my fears to my son, and the desire to control things right along with it. I reinforced the schema of the fantasy of flawlessness in his mind and strengthened the language of perfectionism as his primary mind-set. I taught him that there is no coming back from certain mistakes and that he will be forever haunted by the regret of making them. I taught him that if his errors and missteps create pain and suffering for others, then he has committed the most grievous of wrongs and it can never be reversed. I taught him that I am better at this than he is, and by so doing I placed myself above him, pretending as if I would never make that same mistake or any other mistake like it because I know better and I always take all the necessary precautions to ensure I never get it wrong. He knows this is not true and so do I, but that does not stop me from dangling the fantasy of flawlessness in front of him as the ultimate goal and acting as if I am making more excellent headway toward it than he is.

What a missed opportunity! The chance to practice forgiveness when faced with and hurt by the weakness of others was right there in front of me. Instead of speaking to my son in the language of perfection, in the language of God's love, I spoke to him in the language of flawlessness, and by so doing I decoupled myself from the yoke of Christ and walked the path of selfishness and pride. Only later did it sink in that what was right and what God has commanded of me was to forgive my son and to love him with the love of God, which would have been actualized through that forgiveness.

And yet, it is okay that I failed to forgive my son because that failure, like all failures, provided me with the opportunity to practice repentance for my own stubborn perfectionism, and that repentance if I engage in it yokes me with Christ yet again. You see, we are hopeful and comforted by the prospect of a perfect world, because the opportunities to practice repentance and forgiveness never stop coming. They are an inherent part of our lives. Mistakes, errors, flaws, faults, and yes, even sins and injuries to others, will all accompany us on life's journey. All we have to do, incrementally, here a little and there a little, once in a while, when these things occur, is allow ourselves to accept and embrace our weaknesses and errors and allow God's grace and mercy in, precisely through the very wounds of our errors and our sins, both those we commit and those committed against us by others.

Ride the Waves of Weakness

We both love surfing, so the metaphor of waves crashing on the seashore comes easily to mind at this point. It may be helpful to think of the way of weakness as being like the constant ebb and flow of waves coming to the shore. The waves never stop coming. They may change in size and shape, but they always arrive, and when they do, each wave provides an opportunity for a response. One common response is to try to stand our ground against the waves. We can prove our strength, try to overcompensate for our puniness before these powerful walls of water. We have watched our kids do this, many times. They even pull it off sometimes and cry out exultantly that they have beaten back the waves. But, sure enough, even on a day with smaller surf, every now and again a rogue wave comes along, larger and more powerful than they expected, and it engulfs them and churns them up and knocks them back to the shore. They run to their moms crying, with saltwater running out of their nose and a mouth full of sand. No one who tries to stand strong against the waves gets away without at least a few of these wipeouts.

Another response is to try to keep a safe distance from the waves. We have seen many people who will just dip in a toe here and there. They only let the outermost edges of the waves gently wash up to their feet on the sand. Some work up the courage to move out toward a distant oncoming wave as the water ebbs, only to run as fast as they can away from the wave up the beach as it crashes. These people, too, are often caught off guard by a rogue wave. They don't realize that the tide is changing and that the spot that was once protected and safe is now subject to the full power of the waves. We have seen many children, including our own, miscalculate their position or mistime their escape and get caught by one of these rogue waves. Like the others, they get knocked down, soaking wet, and covered in sand like a churro.

A third response is to move out into the water and learn how to move with the waves instead of fighting or retreating from them. In this response, we learn how to swim with the wave, and in some cases, we can even ride the wave with its power and majesty all the way to the shore. With this third response, we can and will still wipe out, to be sure, but now, rather than try to subdue the ocean and make it bow to our command, or run away from it and never experience the feeling of its movement because of our fear, we submit ourselves to it. We accept its inevitable power. We yield to its superior strength. We embrace it, and we allow ourselves to be taken along with it, sometimes getting glorious rides out of it, sometimes wiping out, and often experiencing both together.

Don't try to stand against weakness. Don't try to fight back the waves of your frailty and your flaws, or those of others. But also, don't run away from weakness and only let it just barely touch your toes. Let the waves of weakness come. Put yourself willingly in their midst. Let them move you back and forth, up and down.

If a weakness engulfs you and throws you down hard, which it will, don't try to compensate by digging your feet deeper into the sand and becoming stronger. Or if, after a bad wipeout, you feel like getting out of the water for good and only letting the very edge of a wave contact you from now on, don't let that fear of weakness control you. Instead, yield to the reality of weakness (your own and those of others) and accept weakness as a necessary and desirable feature of our lives. Give in to frailty and move with the weakness. Let it do what it is designed to do: humble you, make you meek and lowly of spirit and submissive to the Savior. Then, instead of fighting each weakness or trying to run away from weakness, you will learn to ride out each wave of weakness as an opportunity for grace, for love, and for redemption, whether it ends in a wipeout or not.

Practice Weakness Wednesdays

To help us become more accepting of weakness and to practice walking in its way, we encourage a small and simple activity. As a corrective to the traditional format of social media posts, which too often lean toward the fantasy of flawlessness and the language of perfectionism, we ask that you consider on one day of the week, let's say Wednesday, sharing a weakness of yours, rather than a strength; a failure rather than a success; a mistake rather than an achievement; a flaw rather than propped-up perfection. We call this activity "Weakness Wednesdays," and to support your practice of it we have generated several social media sites and groups by this name that can easily be found and joined online.

In the spirit of incremental perfection, we ask that you start small, so that it is not too scary. For example, maybe instead of posting an image of a meal that you successfully and beautifully prepared, you might, just, on Wednesday, share a picture of a meal gone wrong. Or maybe on that day you could share a post acknowledging that even though you already had a good-sized bowl of ice cream for dessert, you went back to the freezer for a second helping. You might admit that you flipped someone the bird after they cut you off on the freeway, only to realize too late that it was a coworker. You could post about the time when you pretended you were asleep and did not hear the baby cry so your spouse would get up and take care of her. You might admit to lying in bed and binge-watching a favorite show for four straight hours instead of doing homework. Share a picture of the dishes in the sink that you let pile up for a week. Whatever it is, try to get a little more comfortable with sharing your weakness, with being exposed and vulnerable, as a sign of your incremental effort to walk the way of weakness. And please do not share other's weaknesses. Only share your own.

This is not a gimmick. We do not ask you to do this to embarrass yourselves. We do not want you to share weakness for weakness' sake. It is, instead, a small step toward a slight shift in our culture. It is a minor movement toward breaking the stranglehold of propped-up perfection and the fantasy of flawlessness. It is an elementary effort toward becoming a little more fluent in the language of perfect love.

If we start to embrace our weaknesses ever so slightly, and if we allow our weaknesses to be exposed to others to even the slightest degree, we begin to change our minds and our hearts. We start to loosen our grip on compensations and overcompensations that lead us always toward the appearance of strength and autonomy. We practice opening the pores that will allow God's grace and love in. We level ourselves with our God, who exemplified and did not hide His walk of weakness, as well as with each other, and we can finally, collectively let our hair down and accept our dependency on our God and each other.

Conclusion

As we walk the way of weakness individually, as families, congregationally, and institutionally, we send a strong message out to the world that lies at the very heart of Christianity and discipleship. This message is abundant in the stories of the Bible we mentioned at the beginning of this book and must always be the guiding principle of our lives. The message is this: We are not and cannot be the saviors of ourselves, for we are weak and we are fallen. We depend completely on Christ for all that we are and all that we can become, and we submit to that dependence by humbly acknowledging and embracing our weakness and by yoking ourselves to Him in repentance and forgiveness. As we repent and forgive, we become level with Him who succors us, and we become level with each other. Then His mercy and His redemptive love can enter into us and into our relationships, and we will love as He loves. And when we love as He loves and when we extend that love outward and help the whole world to love with His love, then we keep Christ's commandment and are, in fact, "therefore perfect, even as our father which is in heaven is perfect."

References

Adler, A. (1927). *Understanding Human Nature*. Center City, Minnesota: Hazelden.

Anderson, R. (1984). Chapter 8: Role of Reader's Schema in Comprehension, Learning, and Memory. *Learning to Read in American Schools*. Hillsdale, NJ: Lawrence Erlbaum Associates, Inc., Publishers.

Bartlett, F.C. (1932). *Remembering: A Study in Experimental and Social Psychology*. Cambridge, England: Cambridge University Press.

Barton, R. (2013). Technology's explosion: The exponential growth rate. Retrieved on June 15th, 2016. http://www.mstech.com/nh-it-blog.php?show=171.

Chambers, O. (2005). Quote retrieved from sermonindex.net on May 22, 2016. http://img.sermonindex.net/modules/newbb/viewtopic_pdf.php?topic_id=8309&forum=45.

Donne, J. (1624). Devotions upon emergent occasions and several steps in my sickness - Meditation XVII.

Dyson, M. (2014). Punishment or Child Abuse? Retrieved on October 15th, 2016. https://www.nytimes.com/2014/09/18/opinion/punishment-or-child-abuse.html?_r=1.

Flynn, J. & Weiss, L. (2007). American IQ gains from 1932 to 2002: The WISC subtests and educational progress. *International Journal of Testing* 7, 209–24.

Frost, R. (2003). As quoted in: The many faces of perfectionism, American Psycological Association. November 2003, vol. 34, no. 10.

Harlow, H. (1958). The nature of love. *American Psychologist,* 13, 673–85.

Howard, J. (2011). Are we addicted to the idea of perfection? Retrieved on June 10, 2016. http://www.huffingtonpost.com/jennifer-howard-phd/beauty-and wisdom_b_954404.html.

Keen, S. (1997). *To love, and be loved.* New York: Bantam Publishing.

Kierkegaard, S. (1991). *Practice in Christianity.* Princeton University Press.

Kurtz, E. & Ketcham, K. (1992). *The Spirituality of Imperfection: Storytelling and the search for meaning.* New York, NY: Bantum Books.

Lewis, C.S. (1952). *Mere Christianity.* New York, NY: HarperCollins Publishers.

Lucyfer (2007, December 6). Re: Be ye therefore perfect—and mentally ill [Online forum comment]. Retrieved from https://www.exmormon.org/mormon/mormon500.htm.

Marano, H.E. (2008). Pitfalls of perfectionism. Retrieved from Psychologytoday.com on June 21, 2015. https://www.psychologytoday.com/articles/200803/pitfalls-perfectionism.

Merton, T. (1966). *Conjectures of a Guilty Bystander.* Garden City, NY: Doubleday.

Miller, K. (2008) Confessions of a former perfectionist. Retrieved from Todayschristianwoman.com on July 25, 2016 at: http://www.todayschristianwoman.com/site/utilities/print.html?type=article&id=58984.

Peoples, S. (2014). God's Purpose in my Child's Disability. Retrieved from http://specialneedsparenting.net/gods-purpose-my-childs-disability/.

Piaget, J. (1923). *"Langage et pensée chez l'enfant"* (3e éd. 1948 revue et avec un nouvel avant-propos et un nouveau chapitre II inséré utgave bind). Neuchâtel: Delachaux et Niestlé, 43f.

Reber, J. & Moody, S. (2013). *Are We Special? The truth and the lie about God's chosen people.* Salt Lake City, UT: Deseret Book Company.

Rich (2013, February 5). Re: Toxic Perfectionism [Blog comment]. Retrieved from https://mormonheretic.org/2013/02/03/toxic-perfectionism/#comment-6846.

Schwartz, M. (2008). The problem with perfection. Retrieved from: https://www.psychologytoday.com/us/blog/shift-mind/200811/the-problem-perfection.

Sturman, E., Flett, G., Hewitt, P., Rudolph, S. (2009). Dimensions of perfectionism and self-worth contingencies in depression. *Journal of Rational-Emotive & Cognitive-Behavior Therapy.*

Too Small? (1935). *Southwestern Union Record*, 34(48), 5.

Younger, K. (2016). Pressing the testimony reset button. Retrieved from: http://sayyesmovement.org/2016/03/pressing-the-reset-button/.

Index

the Lord 18. 40. 41. 47. 48. 54.
62. 63. 64. 69. 71. 72. 73. 74.
75. 76. 79. 85. 86. 105. 124.
131
institutional 130. 131
repentance 4. 5. 20. 21. 35.
50. 75. 76. 79. 127. 131. 135.
136. 139. 141. 145
weakness 2. 4. 5. 6. 11. 44. 45.
47. 48. 49. 50. 56. 63. 78. 83.
84. 101. 105. 107. 120. 121.
122. 123. 124. 126. 130. 131.
132. 134. 135. 137. 138. 139.
140. 141. 143. 144. 145
Isaiah 5. 43. 44. 71. 73. 121
Islam 129

J

Jesus 10. 14. 16. 48. 53. 93. 126.
132
our Shepherd 93
Job 4
John 14. 39. 45. 46. 54. 85. 93. 96.
97. 100. 103. 110
Jonah 4
Judaism 129
Judea 33
judge 4. 53. 65. 67. 79. 111. 134
judgment 35. 53. 70. 71. 113. 121
by God 34. 106. 125. 129
by others 49. 141
judgmental 33. 111

K

Keen, Sam 59. 148
Ketcham, Katherine 39. 148
Kierkegaard, Soren 43. 44. 148
Kurtz, Ernest 39. 148

L

language of perfectionism 8.
22. 26. 38. 55. 60. 62. 70. 72.
81. 84. 103. 112. 114. 121. 130.
131. 134. 139. 140. 143
alternatives to 130
based in fear 93
level 3. 9. 21. 23. 37. 41. 50. 52. 53.
54. 55. 56. 63. 64. 70. 71. 72. 73.
74. 75. 79. 86. 99. 100. 101. 114.
115. 119. 127. 128. 129. 130.
131. 132. 134. 137. 138. 144.
145
Leveling 50
Lewis, C.S. 92. 93. 148
Lincoln, Abraham 117
Lord 117
love v. 5. 11. 12. 14. 16. 40. 41. 42.
43. 45. 46. 47. 48. 49. 50. 51. 55.
56. 57. 59. 60. 61. 62. 63. 67. 68.
70. 71. 72. 73. 75. 76. 77. 78. 79.
83. 85. 86. 96. 97. 98. 99. 100.
101. 104. 105. 106. 107. 108.
109. 110. 111. 112. 115. 123.
124. 125. 126. 127. 128. 129.
130. 131. 132. 133. 134. 135.
136. 137. 138. 139. 140. 141.
143. 144. 145. 148
language of 8. 10. 22. 24. 26.
33. 37. 38. 39. 42. 55. 60. 61.
62. 70. 72. 81. 84. 85. 96. 103.
112. 114. 121. 130. 131. 134.
137. 139. 140. 141. 143. 144
pure divine 110
romanticized 71
lowliness of heart 72

M

authoritarian 91. 92. 94. 95. 97

permissive 93. 94. 95. 97

pastor 84. 85. 107

Paul 5. 45. 46. 47. 48. 49. 50. 63. 66. 84. 104. 105. 106. 110. 111. 115. 123. 124. 127

blameless before the Law 49

Peoples, Sandra 84. 85. 148

perfect v. 1. 2. 3. 6. 7. 8. 10. 11. 12. 13. 14. 15. 16. 17. 18. 19. 20. 22. 27. 28. 29. 31. 32. 33. 34. 35. 39. 40. 41. 42. 43. 45. 46. 47. 48. 50. 55. 59. 61. 62. 67. 72. 73. 74. 75. 77. 79. 83. 85. 86. 96. 97. 99. 100. 101. 103. 104. 105. 106. 110. 123. 126. 127. 128. 130. 131. 132. 133. 134. 137. 138. 139. 141. 144. 145. 148

church 15. 16. 106. 107

commandment to be 12. 16. 17. 18. 19. 20. 22. 32. 39. 41. 42. 46. 55. 103. 104. 126. 127. 132. 137

complete 11. 20. 30. 41. 45. 46. 47. 48. 51. 63. 64. 72. 75. 85. 91. 99. 105. 106. 114. 126. 127. 129. 134

family 3. 6. 14. 60. 85. 86. 88. 100. 113. 114. 115. 119. 122. 137. 139

finished 20. 25. 30. 59. 105

marriage 3. 17. 60. 62. 63. 64. 65. 67. 68. 70. 72. 75. 76. 77. 78. 79

saints vii. 103. 106. 122

whole iv. 2. 3. 20. 40. 41. 45. 46. 47. 48. 49. 55. 57. 63. 64. 75. 76. 78. 85. 86. 88. 94. 99. 105.

106. 107. 109. 111. 115. 120. 123. 126. 127. 133. 134. 145

world 2. 3. 4. 7. 10. 27. 28. 29. 30. 31. 32. 34. 37. 43. 44. 46. 51. 52. 57. 76. 82. 84. 98. 116. 118. 119. 120. 121. 122. 126. 127. 128. 129. 131. 132. 138. 141. 145

perfection 2. 3. 5. 6. 7. 8. 10. 13. 16. 17. 18. 19. 20. 21. 22. 24. 25. 26. 27. 28. 29. 30. 31. 32. 33. 37. 38. 39. 40. 41. 42. 48. 50. 55. 57. 61. 64. 72. 77. 81. 84. 85. 96. 104. 107. 109. 110. 115. 123. 124. 125. 127. 129. 130. 132. 133. 134. 135. 137. 138. 140. 143. 144. 148. 149

achievement of 127

appearance of 3. 121. 129. 138. 144

Christian conception of 10

collective 103. 104. 106. 107. 110

God's love 14. 40. 41. 42. 46. 47. 62. 67. 72. 75. 78. 106. 112. 126. 128. 132. 133. 134. 136. 140

incremental 132. 135

is possible 41. 42. 82. 119. 136. 139

language of 8. 10. 22. 24. 26. 33. 37. 38. 39. 42. 55. 60. 61. 62. 70. 72. 81. 84. 85. 96. 103. 112. 114. 121. 130. 131. 134. 137. 139. 140. 141. 143. 144

pretense of 2. 5. 74. 92. 129. 130. 131

relational 6. 70. 74. 75

Printed in the United States
By Bookmasters